Also by Glenn Liebman

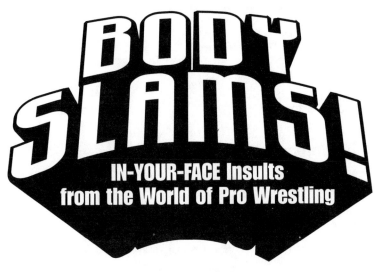

**IN-YOUR-FACE Insults
from the World of Pro Wrestling**

GLENN LIEBMAN

Contemporary Books

*Chicago New York San Francisco Lisbon London Madrid Mexico City
Milan New Delhi San Juan Seoul Singapore Sydney Toronto*

Library of Congress Cataloging-in-Publication Data

Body Slams! : in-your-face insults from the world of pro wrestling /
    [compiled by] Glenn Liebman.
            p.   cm.
        ISBN 0-658-01762-4 (alk. paper)
        1. Wrestling—Humor.   2. Wrestlers—Quotations.   3. Invective.
    I. Liebman, Glenn.

    PN6231.W73 B63   2001
    796.812'02'07—dc21   2001037283

Contemporary Books

A Division of The **McGraw-Hill** Companies

1 2 3 4 5 6 7 8 9 0   LBM/LBM   0 9 8 7 6 5 4 3 2 1

ISBN 0-658-01762-4

This book was set in Stone Informal
Printed and bound by Lake Book Manufacturing

Interior design by Nick Panos
Interior photographs: page vi, The Rock © Duomo/CORBIS; page viii, Kane ©
Duomo/CORBIS; page x, Goldberg © Duomo/CORBIS; page 232, "Stone Cold"
Steve Austin © Michael Brennan/CORBIS; page 246, Jesse Ventura © Reuters
Newmedia Inc./CORBIS

McGraw-Hill books are available at special quantity discounts to use as premiums
and sales promotions, or for use in corporate training programs. For more
information, please write to the Director of Special Sales, Professional Publishing,
McGraw-Hill, Two Penn Plaza, New York, NY 10121-2298. Or contact your local
bookstore.

This book is printed on acid-free paper.

To Frankie—my favorite wrestling buddy and legendary body slammer

ENTS

ACKNOWL

DGMENTS

I would like to thank my editor, Denise Betts, who has been wonderful to work with on this book as well as all the other Slams! and Sports Shorts projects we have done together. I hope there will be many more in the future!

A special thanks to Frankie, who is a wonderful son and a great pal, and my wife, Kathy, who will always be my best friend and tag-team partner.

INTROD

UCTION

"**N**ow entering the ring, from the great state of Illinois, the notorious Log Splitter himself, Abraham "Stove Top" Lincoln!"

OK, so they didn't have colorful ring announcers in the mid-1800s, but our 16th president was a wrestler. Maybe ol' Abe didn't have the fuchsia tights and booming entrance music, but there is no doubt he could have cut one helluva promo.

Wrestling has been a part of our lives for more than two millennia. But tracing the history of pro wrestling as we know it today—the drama, the high-risk aerobatics, the heels and babyfaces—is almost as complicated as defining the exact beginning of man.

In 1877, William Muldoon defeated the French champion to be named the first professional World Wrestling Champion. Most wrestling fans sitting at home wearing their Hulkamania bandannas probably never heard of him, but he is the "Fertile Crescent" for a long line of legends—names like Bruno Sammartino, "Nature Boy" Buddy Rogers, Dusty Rhodes, the Von Erichs, Classy Freddie Blassie, The Fabulous Moolah, Killer Kowalski, Gorgeous George, Ed "Strangler" Lewis, Rikidozan, Andre the Giant, King Kong Bundy, Iron Sheik, and Ted DiBiase.

These stars evolved from small promotions to national fame and sometimes fortune. For every Hulk Hogan there's a kid in Nebraska busting his butt to make $25 for a match in the local high school gym—and he had to drive more than 100 miles to get there. Only recently could you expect to make big bank once you reach the top; before, you had to settle for a little cash and lots of appreciation and devotion from dedicated, enthusiastic fans.

Those fans have been fueling the industry for years. Regional promotions (or wrestling organizations) packed them into places such as the aforementioned gym, veterans' halls, church basements, fairgrounds, farms, anywhere you could pound down the ring posts and throw up some stands for folks to sit in. Promotions became as competitive with each other as their champs did with their opponents, and slowly organizations merged.

In 1948, the National Wrestling Alliance was formed; this was an umbrella organization for North American promotions, and Lou Thesz was its first champion. The NWA wasn't the only combination of efforts by promotions, but unlike the others, the NWA has a living legacy. It still exists, still puts butts in the seats for small and big towns alike, but its creation eventually spawned the Big Three—World Wrestling Federation, World Championship Wrestling, and Extreme Championship Wrestling.

The World Wrestling Federation, the big daddy of promotions, was born when Vince McMahon bought Capitol Championship Wrestling from his father, Vince Sr., in 1982. In part of McMahon Sr.'s territory was the World Wide Wrestling Federation, an organization of northeastern promoters who broke off from the NWA after a title dispute. WCW sprang from the loins of the NWA, and its heavyweight title was renamed the World Championship Wrestling World Heavyweight title. After its split from the NWA, the WCW was purchased by billionaire bad boy Ted Turner. Then, ECW, then known as Eastern Championship Wrestling, flew the coop and changed its name in 1994.

Pro wrestling became sports entertainment, and a whole new breed of wrestler was unleashed on the world. Wrestling is all over the media. Andy Kaufman's bid to be the Intergender Champion and getting into a program with Jerry "The King" Lawler brought Hollywood to wrestling; Cyndi Lauper spurred on the rock-n-wrestling connection when she managed Wendi Richter at the first Wrestlemania. The marriage between wrestling and television, which had been decades old by then, is stronger than ever. Shows like *Saturday Night's Main Event*, *Monday Night Nitro*, *Smackdown!*, and *Thunder*, as well as local promotions' weekly televised events, have introduced fans to the likes of Rowdy Roddy Piper, Stone Cold Steve Austin, Captain Lou Albano, and Goldberg. Wrestling stars showed up in movies (Hogan, Andre the Giant, Piper); mainstream celebrities appeared in the squared circle (New York Giant Lawrence Taylor, Mr. T., Pete Rose).

So what's next, now that ECW has filed for bankruptcy and McMahon has won the Battle of the Billionaires by purchasing WCW? Is there only one game in town?

Just ask the kid in Nebraska taking bumps and icing down his bruises while paying dues in a one-stoplight town. To him there's another night in another town, probably another 40 miles away. But when he shows up, there will be 10 or 50 or 500 dedicated, passionate, and rabid fans waiting for him to somersault off the ropes, maybe spill a little hardway juice, and inspire them to spring out of their seats. All across the country and around the world, regional promotions are keeping the desire for human combat and drama alive and well. And who knows . . . maybe they are watching the next Abraham Lincoln.

THE ACOLYTES

"The Acolytes like to do two things—drink beer and
fight. They do both very well."

—Michael Cole

"The Acolytes' forte is no-holds-barred. You know why?
They don't know any holds."

—Kevin Kelly, on the Acolytes' fighting style

"They're the kind of guys who make a big pledge to the
Jerry Lewis telethon and then don't send the money in."

—Jerry Lawler, on the Acolytes

"They're tougher than a three-dollar steak."

—Jim Ross

ADVERSARIES

"Do unto others whatever you think is funny."
—*Jerry Lawler, quoting from his own commandments*

"I fought Bruno [Sammartino] so many times in so many cities that it all kind of blends together."
—*Gorilla Monsoon, a man with the memory of an elephant*

"Rooty-poo candy-asses."
—*The Rock, talking tough about his opponents*

LOU ALBANO

"I was never a great wrestler. I did mostly running."
—*Lou Albano, a modest, or maybe realistic, man*

"Often imitated but never duplicated."

—*Lou Albano, his famous trademark line*

"A fat bag of wind."

—*Cyndi Lauper, on Lou, who appeared as her dad*
in the video "Girls Just Wanna Have Fun"

OLE ANDERSON

"He's as strong as an ox . . . and almost as smart."

—*Rowdy Roddy Piper, referring to a man never*
destined to be the valedictorian

ANDRE THE GIANT

"I swear he drank 100 beers one night."

—*Terry Funk, on the Giant's high*
tolerance and huge appetite

"He's 7'4" and over 500 pounds. If he didn't want to lose, he wasn't going to lose."

—Hulk Hogan, calling it like it is

KURT ANGLE

"To compare an Olympic gold medalist with a black belt in martial arts would be somewhat degrading to my many, many accomplishments."

—Kurt Angle, Olympic gold medal winner, on wrestling against black belt Steve Blackman

"A conniving, double-talking, sniveling liar."

—Mick Foley, no fan of Angle's

"I wanna apologize to all the Jeriholics who had to listen to another one of your boring, long-winded speeches."

—Chris Jericho, to Angle about his extended mike time (or was it Clinton's State of the Union address?)

"Y2J has an *I* of his own—I wish that you would shut the hell up!"

> —*Chris Jericho, infringing on Angle's trademark three Is*

"An Olympic hero with no neck."

> —*Chris Jericho, on Angle's stumpy appearance*

"This is not the Olympics. You're not facing the Romanians, you're not facing the Bulgarians, you're facing the Rock."

> —*The Rock, unintentionally insulting the Romanians and Bulgarians, along with Angle, by placing himself in their company*

"I'm thinking about beating the Olympic mucus from out of your smug, smiling face."

> —*The Rock, to Angle, showing off his extensive vocabulary by using the technical term for "snot"*

"Stick it straight up your Olympic ass."
>   —*The Rock, to Kurt Angle, on what he would*
>   *do with Angle's gold medal*

KURT ANGLE PHILOSOPHY

"I have the three *Is*—intensity, integrity, and intelligence."
>   —*Kurt Angle, his trademark line*

"As all of you know, I am the most celebrated real athlete in WWF history."
>   —*Kurt Angle, showing he's yet another person*
>   *who fails to recognize the athletic*
>   *achievements of Captain Lou Albano*

TONY ATLAS

"He looks like the south end of a northbound turkey."
—*Bobby Heenan, on Atlas*

STONE COLD STEVE AUSTIN

"Foulmouthed, beer-drinking, trash-talking, poor role model for children everywhere."
—*Kurt Angle, describing not only Austin, but also most of the pro wrestling characters*

"The Rock's saying he sends chill bumps down the arms of Stone Cold Steve Austin. . . . There ain't a man alive that sends a chill bump down my arm."
—*Stone Cold Steve Austin*

"That man is dumber than a bag of rocks."
—*Stone Cold Steve Austin, on a scholarly opponent*

"Steve Austin is the kind of guy who would shoot at the welcome wagon."

> —*Jerry Lawler, pouring out his affection for Austin*

"Stone Cold's at home with a beer in his hand . . . and a beer in his other hand."

> —*Jerry Lawler, on Stone Cold's balanced diet*

"There is no depth that I will not stoop to to make your life here on earth a total complete living hell."

> —*Vince McMahon, spoken like the true villain he is*

"I haven't gotten the stench out of my office yet."

> —*Vince McMahon, after Austin was temporary CEO of the WWF and used McMahon's office*

"All that hard work, 50 cents couldn't buy you a cup of redneck coffee."

> —*The Rock, serving up trash at the Redneck Café*

"I can take your rotting soul anytime I wish."
—*The Undertaker, staying true to
the spirit of his name*

"I hate everyone—but your name is on top of the list."
—*The Undertaker, complimenting Stone Cold
on making it to the top of the list*

"I haven't seen a redneck drive that fast since they took
Dukes of Hazzard off the air."
—*X-Pac, seeing Stone Cold Steve Austin drive by*

BOB BACKLUND

"He was a paperboy in Mayberry, used to sweep the
floors for Floyd."
—*Bobby Heenan, on Backlund's
all-American-boy image*

BAD GUYS

"Titles do no good on good guys."
>—*Animal, of the Legion of Doom's Road Warriors*

"I know there's a lot of snakes in the WWF, but most of them are of the two-legged variety."
>—*Jerry Lawler*

"I've always been a snake. I've always been cruel but fair."
>—*Jake Roberts, introducing himself to Jerry Lawler*

"Getting people mad enough to pay to see me get my ass kicked."
>—*Jesse Ventura, on his goal as a pro wrestler.*
>*(He used the same strategy to get himself elected governor of Minnesota.)*

JOHNNY B. BADD

"He's colder than a mother-in-law's kiss."
> —*Bobby Heenan, after Johnny B. Badd was*
> *knocked out by Stone Cold Steve Austin*

BUFF BAGWELL

"Nobody puts his hands on one of the most dynamic
men the wrestling world has ever seen."
> —*Buff Bagwell, on Eric Bischoff grabbing Bagwell*

"Buff is the stuff."
> —*Buff Bagwell, his trademark motto*

"Cream Puff Bagwell."
> —*Hulk Hogan, a poet who didn't even know it*

BASEBALL

"I'm trying to be the Cal Ripken of wrestling."

—Mick Foley, on missing only four matches in three years

"If the Cubs hit like that, they'd be in first place."

—Bobby Heenan, on a no-holds-barred fight in Chicago during an atrocious losing streak by the Cubbies

"You received seven thousand votes to get into the Hall of Fame. You'd have gotten a lot more, but you ran out of stamps."

—Bobby Heenan, all-around sports authority, to Bob Uecker

"Can you smell what I'm cookin'?"

—Mike Piazza, asked what he should have said to Roger Clemens after Clemens beaned him. (It's the Rock's trademark line.)

"No, someone could get hurt."

—*Mike Piazza, asked if he practiced any of his childhood wrestling moves on his fellow Mets. He has a WWF career waiting for him when he retires from baseball.*

"When you want to go one-on-one with Russo, I'll jack you higher than your ERA."

—*Vince Russo to John Rocker, who was rumored to be considering wrestling Russo*

"Everyone wants to see the WCW mentality on the arena floor where they're at, be it hockey, baseball, basketball, or football."

—*Mike Schmidt, on the instant offense in sports today, especially baseball*

"With the Cardinals, everyone would be reading the business section to see what their stocks were doing. Here, you get to the locker room in the morning and everybody is looking at the sports page to see if Hulk Hogan won."

> —Andy Van Slyke, after being traded from the Cardinals to the Pirates, on the differences in priorities between the two teams

PAUL BEARER

"This is what you get when you cross the line into a realm of darkness."

> —Paul Bearer, maintaining a positive attitude as he attempts to embalm Stone Cold

"Looks like a well-kept grave."

> —Jerry Lawler, on Bearer's chiseled face

"Paul Bearer is so fat, he has his own gravitational pull."

—*Jerry Lawler*

"He always has that eerie smell of formaldehyde."

—*Gorilla Monsoon, commenting on Bearer's cologne*

BEEFCAKE

"He's like a refrigerator. Let's hang some magnets and the grocery list on him."

—*Bobby Heenan, presenting alternative uses for Beefcake*

"It sounds like a trip to the hardware store. I can hear the screw move."

—*Bobby Heenan, said as Beefcake's face was being pounded by an opponent*

BELT

"The belt looks like cuff links to O'Neal."
> —*Bobby Heenan, on Shaquille O'Neal holding the
> WCW title belt. Shaquille the Giant
> does have a certain ring to it.*

"Stay away from my belt or I'll skin your ass and make
a pair of boots out of them."
> —*Jeff Jarrett, to Stone Cold Steve Austin*

"You can't even fit it around your chubby gut."
> —*Chris Jericho, watching Big Show struggle to put
> on the WWF title belt around his baby fat*

"There's not one belt he wouldn't hit below."
> —*Jerry Lawler, on Marc Mero, who is known for
> hitting below the belt*

"The sight of it on him makes me physically ill—makes me wanna vomit."

—Vince McMahon, on Steve Austin
wearing the title belt

"It's not your belt I want—it's your ass that holds it up that I want."

—Road Dogg, to Val Venis, although he'd
probably take the belt too

"I bust my ass for years to get that title, and that jackass just has one handed to him."

—Triple H, on Arnold Schwarzenegger being given
an honorary championship belt. Perhaps if Triple H
were a megamillion-dollar blockbuster movie star
he wouldn't have to work so hard for the belt.

"Each and every one of you can rest assured that every single time I hold this in the air, you can kiss my ass."

—Triple H, said respectfully to his coworkers and
fans while he was holding high the title belt

CHRIS BENOIT

"I'm the greatest technical wrestler in the world today and the greatest technical wrestler in the history of the WWF."

—Chris Benoit, the most modest technical
wrestler in the world today

"I'd rather go down to the San Diego Zoo, dressed like a pork chop, and jump in the lion's pen."

—Bobby Heenan, on the prospect of
having to wrestle Chris Benoit

"You may run into a wall—after you experience the Walls of Jericho."

—Chris Jericho, a man proficient in his biblical
references, about wrestling Chris Benoit

"A gap-toothed robot."

—Chris Jericho, on Benoit's lack of charisma

"Benoit in French means gap-toothed jackass."

—*Chris Jericho*

BEVERAGE OF CHOICE

"I'll come back and beat your ass, and drink a case of
beer in the process."

—*Stone Cold Steve Austin, to Vince McMahon*

"Does anybody have a cold beer for Stone Cold?"

—*Stone Cold Steve Austin, one of his rallying cries*

"Depends on how much beer I drink."

—*Stone Cold Steve Austin, asked
how long his matches last*

"Why don't you drink a big, tall glass of shut-up juice."

—*The Rock, to an opponent*

BIG BOSSMAN

"You stuck your hand in the Big Bossman's business. Nobody, but nobody, does that to me."
> —*Big Bossman, threatening the British Bulldog*

"I think it's about time you did some hard time, punk."
> —*Big Bossman, to an opponent*

"Y2J is telling you, if you can't say anything entertaining, then shut the hell up."
> —*Chris Jericho, on the mike time of Big Bossman*

"Can't even believe him when he says he's lying."
> —*Jerry Lawler, on the honesty and integrity of Big Bossman*

"I will stuff this rancid sock that looks a lot like me down the gullet of the Bossman, because I can."
> —*Mankind, displaying his healthy self-image*

BIG POPPA PUMP

"Women and riding my Harley."
>—*Big Poppa Pump, describing his and a million*
>*American men's two favorite things*

"Doing what I do best: beat people up and give 'em a good hooching."
>—*Big Poppa Pump, on the only*
>*other thing he likes to do*

BIG SHOW

"Big Freak Show."
>—*Big Bossman. (It takes one to know one.)*

"He couldn't organize a one-car parade."
>—*Bradshaw, on the organizing*
>*capabilities of Big Show*

"What you deserve to be doing is carrying my bags into the arena."

> —Chris Jericho, to Big Show, which goes to show
> that he's not only an Olympic medal winner,
> he's also a prima donna

"What matters is charisma and sportsmanship, both of which you have absolutely none of."

> —Chris Jericho, to Big Show

"Everybody looks up to the Big Show, and that's actually because he just knocked them down."

> —Jerry Lawler, friend (for the moment) of Big Show

"I guess if you're 7'2" and you weigh 500 pounds, it don't make any difference."

> —Jerry Lawler, on whom Big Show would fight

"Pathetic, pea-brained waste of perfectly good oxygen."

> —Shane McMahon, on Big Show

"He isn't as quick on the uptake as you or me."
>—*Vince McMahon, said to the Rock about Big Show*

"That's ten pounds of monkey crap in a five-pound bag."
>—*The Rock, on Big Show*

"Every Rock fan stops, pauses, and takes a look, and they all say this: 'I'm going to take a leak—this guy sucks.'"
>—*The Rock, on Big Show's time at the mike. But when you gotta go, you gotta go!*

"A 7', 500-pound, steaming, stinking pile of grade-A monkey crap."
>—*The Rock, who finally got his calculations right, if not the substance*

"When you insult the Great One, when you insult the people's champion, you insult the people."
>—*The Rock, retaliating from some smack from Big Show*

"I would bash his pea brain with a sledgehammer already."

—Triple H. If he had a hammer,
he'd hammer the Big Show.

"I lay your big goofy ass down . . . and you stare up at the ceiling for a big one, two, three."

—Triple H, on what he would do to
the Big Show during a heat

BIG SHOW PHILOSOPHY

"I am the biggest, nastiest bastard to ever set foot in the WWF, and I am damn proud of it."

—Big Show, who seems to share
others' opinions of himself

"The most dominating force that has ever walked in the WWF."

—Big Show. (Have we heard that one before?)

"You wanna know why nobody likes me? Because all of you can never be 7'2", 500 pounds. It drives you absolutely nuts."

> —Big Show, who can't seem to understand
> that nobody wants to be like him

ERIC BISCHOFF

"I'm not gonna punch you . . . because I don't have another two million bucks."

> —Ric Flair, explaining that he wasn't going to hit
> Bischoff for fear he would be sued—again

"Even a man like Ted Turner makes a few mistakes along the way, and you're one of them."

> —Ric Flair, to Bischoff. (Another would be
> selling the WCW to Shane McMahon.)

"Estrogen Boy."

> —Kevin Nash, citing what Bischoff's momma used
> to say to call him home for dinner

"Remember Baltimore, weatherman? I stuck you once, and I can't wait to stick you again."

> —Kevin Nash, telling former weatherman Bischoff that there were cloudy skies ahead

"Sleazy-E, that little squirm of a worm."

> —Diamond Dallas Page, rapping about Bischoff

STEVE BLACKMAN

"Steve, you will never ever have the talent or charisma of Y2J."

> —Chris Jericho, who took on the cumbersome nickname of Y2JI for 2001

"Blackman's got the personality of lint."

> —Jerry Lawler

"He had a charisma bypass."

> —Jerry Lawler, on Blackman

"I'll let you know when I find your charisma."
>—*Mankind, helping his friend Blackman*
>*locate his charisma*

"If you think you have a personality, maybe someday you'll eventually get one."
>—*Al Snow, playing the song "Personality"*
>*to Blackman, whose motto is*
>*"I think I can, I think I can . . ."*

"Mick Foley had three personalities—you've got no personality."
>—*Al Snow, wondering what's better: no personality*
>*or one in which you are a rancid sock?*

FREDDIE BLASSIE

"The guy I see every time I look in the mirror."
>—*Freddie Blassie, asked who was the*
>*toughest wrestler of his era*

"I was the most hated fella. If I didn't win as the most hated, I'd felt like I failed in my mission in life."
—*Freddie Blassie, explaining his emotions when the most hated wrestler was announced every year*

BODY PARTS

"He got real squashed. Thank God ribs are flexible."
—*Bam Bam Bigelow, on cleaning the plate with his opponent*

"I have never been in a position where somebody has asked me to put my body on the line. I have always offered it."
—*Mick Foley, on giving his all for his career*

"I don't go around measuring my arms. I just use them."
—*Goldberg, insulted by inane questions about his arms' length*

"They told me to watch my mouth on Sunday Night
Heat, but my damn nose is in the way."

—*Road Dogg*

BOOK CLUB

"I read your book and couldn't even get by the
Introduction."

—*D-Generation X, on Mankind's bestselling
autobiography,* Have a Nice Day

"The only reason anybody bought your book in the first
place is they were hoping you would die at the end of
it."

—*Chris Jericho, on Mankind's book, which doesn't
have the happy ending he had hoped for*

"I'm waiting for the Cliff's Notes."

—*Jerry Lawler, on Mankind's book*

"Maybe if you're out of toilet paper, you could use a couple of the pages."

—Jerry Lawler, after saying Mankind's book was good bathroom reading

"It's not written in crayon, is it?"

—Jerry Lawler, hoping Mankind's book was written in his favorite writing implement

"Lots of pictures to color in there."

—Jerry Lawler, on failing to understand that coloring books and autobiographical books are two entirely different things

"Kane won't even read a book unless it's got the words 'Chicken Soup' in the title."

—Jerry Lawler, on X-Pac helping to show the world the sensitive side of Kane

"I can't thank the magazines and the newspapers, because it's beneath them to read a book that a pro wrestler wrote."

> —*Mankind, thanking people for making his book the top seller in the country*

"It's gonna be real difficult for me to come out here and thank all the book critics, because they're too damn stupid to read it themselves."

> —*Mankind, on thanking the critics for making his book a number one seller*

"I hope Frank McCourt doesn't take it too hard."

> —*Mankind, when his book passed Frank McCourt's* Angela's Ashes *to become the number one seller in the country*

BOSTON

"If you follow my three *Is*, then maybe someday even this town could win a World Series."
                    —*Kurt Angle, to WWF fans in Boston*

"There's something about this town that inspires its athletes to greatness—once they leave, of course."
                    —*Kurt Angle*

"It's a dump. I froze in the winter, and I sweated to death over the summer."
                    —*Gorilla Monsoon, on Boston Garden*

BOXING

"The trouble with boxing is that it lacks credibility."
                    —*Vince McMahon*

BRADSHAW

"Thou shalt not drink our beer."

*—Bradshaw, citing one of the commandments
of the Acolytes. He might as well
tell this to Stone Cold.*

"I'm gonna break your legs, and I'm gonna break your spirit—and then when I'm through with all that, then I'm gonna beat the crap out of you some more."

*—Ken Shamrock, a man who evidently doesn't
know the meaning of "going too far"*

BRITISH BULLDOG

"I am gonna knock the Brahma bullcrap out of you."

—British Bulldog, to the Rock

"How about we see if your bite is as bad as your bark."

*—Chyna, to the British Bulldog, before
she made him look like a poodle*

D'LO BROWN

"Like me or hate me, you'd better learn to live with me, because I'm not going anywhere."

—*D'Lo Brown*

KING KONG BUNDY

"The walking condominium."

—*Gorilla Monsoon, on the yuppie's choice of wrestler*

BUSHWHACKERS

"Luke is so dumb, if they were twins, he wouldn't know when his brother's birthday was."

—*Bobby Heenan*

"The bad thing about the Bushwhackers is that—win, lose, or draw—you gotta have everything you got on fumigated."

—*Bobby Heenan, talking about the Bushwhackers' pungent odor*

"The Bushwhackers are living proof that the Three Stooges had children."

—*Gorilla Monsoon*

CACTUS JACK

"I can't jump so high, so I jump from high places."

—*Cactus Jack, who wouldn't have made a good basketball player*

"Get somebody down here. The rail could be damaged."

—*Bobby Heenan, on Cactus Jack crashing into the railing at a wrestling match*

"When he dies, he'll have to rent mourners."

—Jerry Lawler, on Cactus Jack's arid friendships

"Calling Cactus Jack stupid is an insult to stupid people."

—Jerry Lawler

"My dream, Cactus Jack, is to be in the WWF without you in it."

—Triple H, after Cactus Jack told him his dream is to be WWF champion

CELL MATCHES

"Too many Hell in a Cell matches for him."

—Jerry Lawler, on Mankind's appearance and mental state

"The only match where winning is secondary to surviving."

—The Undertaker, on the dangerous and deadly cell matches

CHAINSAW CHARLIE

"If he had a brain, he'd be an idiot."

—Jerry Lawler, on Chainsaw Charlie

CHAMP

"If you aren't in the WWF to be the champ, you got no business being here at all."

—Stone Cold Steve Austin

"You got a real champion. No more Barbie doll lipstick losers."

—Ivory, on being the women's WWF champion

"WWF has always been about honor and integrity—qualities that are sorely lacking in our current WWF champion."

—Vince McMahon, on Stone Cold
Steve Austin. (Huh?)

"Hell hath no fury [greater] than what you would do if you interfere in the WWF championship."

—Vince McMahon, warning the Undertaker not to
interfere in a championship match

"To be the best, you have got to beat the best. To be the WWF champion, you have got to beat me."

—Triple H

"The fact of the matter is you can line 'em up and I'll roll 'em down, from the bottom all the way up."

—Triple H, as WWF champion and
previous pro bowling champ

"A win is a win, and when it comes to the WWF title, I'll take it any way I can get it."

—*Triple H, on winning the championship against Mankind with the help of the referee*

CHEATING

"I am not a cheater. I am not the Minnesota Timberwolves of the WWF."

—*Kurt Angle, referring to the secret contract the Timberwolves had with basketball star Joe Smith*

"I can't win a match unless I cheat. And people love me."

—*Hulk Hogan, on his bad-guy image and his millions of adoring fans*

"Cheating is only cheating when you get caught."

—*Jerry Lawler, no stickler for dictionary definitions*

"Win if you can, lose if you must, but always cheat."
—*Jesse Ventura, words of advice to pro wrestlers and politicians alike*

CHOKE HOLD

"He left more wrestlers choked up than *Old Yeller*."
—*Ken Hoffman*, Houston Chronicle, *on Lord Alfred Hayes's choke hold*

"He's all choked up."
—*Jerry Lawler, on the Rock choking Mankind (pun intended)*

CHRISTIAN AND EDGE

"Can you smell it? That's us—totally reeking of awesomeness."
—*Christian and Edge, on wrestling and beating the Rock while not wearing deodorant*

CHYNA

"Her biceps suggest she could bench-press Vermont."
—*David Casstevens,* Arizona Republic *columnist*

"This is no place for a woman. So you got two choices—
you either get your ass up or get your ass out of this
ring."
—*Hardcore Holly, trying to rouse Chyna*

"You have no business being in the ring with any man,
let alone the greatest International Champion of all
time."
—*Jeff Jarrett, to Chyna before she showed him
that girls aren't made of sugar and spice
and everything nice*

"An inspiration to millions of women, children, and
idiots across the nation."
—*Chris Jericho, on Chyna as a symbol
of women's liberation*

"You are one bad mamma jamma."

> —*Chris Jericho, giving Chyna his usual*
> *one compliment a year*

"The Yoko Ono of DX."

> —*Jerry Lawler, on Chyna breaking up*
> *the boys' club in pro wrestling*

"When she comes into a room, mice jump on chairs."

> —*Jerry Lawler, admiring how Chyna turns the*
> *tables on the stereotypes of women*

CHYNA PHILOSOPHY

"I saw myself as the first woman ass-kicker."

> —*Chyna, the original Xena Warrior Princess,*
> *speaking of her childhood self-image*

"Women are not trying to look like Barbie anymore. They're trying to look like Chyna."

—Chyna, a woman with the same proportions as Barbie's evil twin

CLOTHES MAKE THE MAN

"I no longer need my power tie, because I always have my power finger."

—Stone Cold Steve Austin, on flipping the bird to Vince McMahon

"The bottom line is if he takes it to another level, I'll hold on to his panty hose."

—Hulk Hogan, admiring the dashing dress Dennis Rodman wore in the ring

"[Tonga Kid's] outfit made him look like a Don Ho roadie."

—Tony Kornheiser

"Triple H may wear the pants in the family, but I think Stephanie tells him what pants to wear."

> *—Jerry Lawler, on the blissful marriage of Triple H and Stephanie McMahon*

"Whatever it is, a whole herd of them were wiped out to make it."

> *—Jerry Lawler, asked what the less-than-svelte Viscera's jacket was made of*

"Where did you get that suit from? Did the man at the carnival guess your weight wrong?"

> *—Jerry Lawler, to Tiny Tim, attending a WWF event in sartorial splendor*

MICHAEL COLE

"You're embarrassing yourself and those around you."

> *—Christian, about a Michael Cole interview*

"You are the most inefficient, unequivocally worst announcer I've ever seen."

—*Chris Jericho, on the talents of Cole*

"She's not your type. She's not inflatable."

—*Jerry Lawler, admiring Michael Cole's appeal to women of all shapes, sizes, and materials*

"There's actually one too many of us out here at this broadcast table, and I think it's you."

—*Jerry Lawler, to his sole companion, Michael Cole*

"Shut your mouth or I will slap the taste out of you."

—*The Rock, to Cole*

"Well, Michael, the Rock is thinking about slamming the yellow off your teeth."

—*The Rock*

CONTENDERS TO THE THROWN

"Wait till the Big Bossman takes care of the rest of the morons in the WWF."

> —*Big Bossman, on taking on all contenders and WWF geniuses*

"You haven't paid your dues, Mankind, Mick Foley, Cactus Jack, Dude Love, whatever the hell your name is—if you even know."

> —*Vince McMahon, denying Mankind a title match and acknowledging his identity crisis*

JIM CORNETTE

"I can beat anyone, either male, female, animal, vegetable, or mineral."

> —*Jim Cornette, after a deadly winning match against a tossed salad*

CROTCH SHOTS

"If you had to kick someone in the groin, you'd kick 'em in the groin."

—Freddie Blassie, giving an example of his honest philosophy

"It's the best way to bring 'em down."

—Chyna, on why she kicks guys in the gonads

"There probably won't be any more little Als running around."

—Jerry Lawler, after Al Snow was hit hard in the family jewels

"Hit in the south side of the Dogg pound."

—Jim Ross, describing how Road Dogg was hit below the championship belt

DC

"I'm America's role model. I need to go inside and see the chief."

—Chris Jericho, in Washington, trying to get into the White House

"We're in the nation's capital—you can't do that."

—Jerry Lawler, after the Rock pulled down his pants during a match in Washington

DETROIT

"Unlike this town, your Olympic hero will bounce back, overcome adversity, and be your champion once again."

—Kurt Angle, trashing the Motor City

D-GENERATION X

"D-Generation are a bunch of damn pigs."
> —*Michael Cole, describing the enormous*
> *appeal of D-Generation X*

"D-Generation X will be your judge, your jury, your executioner."
> —*D-Generation X, describing the wrestling*
> *legal system to Vince McMahon*

"You guys are like the Bad News Bears of the WWF."
> —*Shane McMahon, to those cute rugrats, D-Gen X*

"What, do we have a loser convention in town?"
> —*Shane McMahon, referring to the*
> *gruesome twosome*

DUDE LOVE

"The psychedelic jackass."

> —*Stone Cold Steve Austin, on the hippie*
> *with an identity crisis*

"The hippest cat in the world."

> —*Dude Love, one cool dude*

BUH BUH RAY DUDLEY

"Buh Buh Ray's a couple of fries short of a Happy
Meal."

> —*Kevin Kelly, who is no Biggie Size himself*

"They'd knock his brains out—if he had any."

> —*Jerry Lawler, on what Christian and Edge*
> *would do to Buh Buh*

DUDLEYS

"The Dudleys are going to get the VIP treatment—very intense pain."

—*Jerry Lawler, the ultimate host*

HACKSAW DUGGAN

"He's a brain donor."

—*Bobby Heenan, on Duggan*

"With Duggan, taking a shower is a high-risk maneuver."

—*Bobby Heenan*

"He's at a disadvantage when he wakes up."

—*Bobby Heenan, after an announcer said Duggan was disadvantaged in the coming match*

ECW

"The WWF needs ECW like Michael Jordan needs Head and Shoulders."

> —*Jerry Lawler, on the horrifying possibility of a merger between the WWF and the ECW*

"Bunch of has-beens working out of some bingo hall in Philadelphia."

> —*Jerry Lawler, on the notoriously high level of wrestling found in the ECW*

EDGE

"If you put a nickel on his head, he'd look like a nail."

> —*Jerry Lawler, on Edge being a bag of bones*

FABULOUS MOOLAH

"I want to thank you for saving me a trip to the
museum to see what my ancestors looked like."
—Ivory, to the aging and ageless Moolah

"I heard your birthday suit needs a little ironing."
—Jerry Lawler, shuddering at the thought

"Moolah's birth certificate was in hieroglyphics."
—Jerry Lawler

"If I told Moolah to act her age, she'd die."
*—Jerry Lawler, not realizing that Moolah's
like Dick Clark—she'll never die*

"She was a waitress at the Last Supper."
—Jerry Lawler

"Ivory told Moolah to wrestle women her own age, but there aren't any."

—*Jerry Lawler*

FAMILY MCMAHON

"She may find out he's the sap."
—*Jerry Lawler, urging Stephanie McMahon to find out more about Test's family roots before marrying him*

"Why don't the two of you just go ahead and book yourself on the Jerry Springer show and get it over with?"
—*Vince McMahon, on the sibling rivalry between Shane and Stephanie*

"You don't screw with McMahon's family."
—*Jim Ross, citing one of the unwritten rules of the WWF*

"Not only am I marrying the greatest girl in the world, I'm marrying the greatest family in the world, too."

—Test, on what he thought was his impending marriage to Stephanie McMahon and the joyous years that lay ahead

"If you mess with us, you've got two choices. You either get your ass kicked or you get your ass fired."

—Triple H, who along with his wife, Stephanie McMahon, is in charge of the WWF

FAN CLUB

"All of you people here are used to that—falling short of your goals and dreams time after time—and that's expected. But for me, it's different."

—Kurt Angle, on his disappointment after losing a match

"The people here don't have much to live for."

—Kurt Angle, on WWF fans

"I raise a standard of excellence that you and the people here tonight can only dream of achieving."
—*Kurt Angle, to the Rock and his fans*

"Ladies and gentlemen . . . and I use that term loosely."
—*Bob Backlund, addressing some of his fans*

"You're too weak. You can't go on a diet for more than one day."
—*Bob Backlund, slamming puny fans of pro wrestling*

"If you could live under my standards, we would have . . . a perfect world."
—*Bob Backlund, raising the bar*

"I'm not the one who's an asshole—it's all of you."
—*Big Bossman, responding to derogatory chants from the crowd*

"Pencil-necked geeks."
—*Freddie Blassie, on the members of his ex-fan club*

"The thing that scares me about wrestling fans is that they can vote and they can breed."

> —Bobby Heenan, biting off the
> whole arm that feeds him

"I promise to never, ever treat you Jeriholics wrong, just because I am better than all of you."

> —Chris Jericho, to his many fans

"I would describe it as a Jeriholics euphoria and ambrosia."

> —Chris Jericho, on his fans going wild
> for him in New York City

"We gave them an IQ test and the results came back negative."

> —Jerry Lawler, referring to some WWF fans

"I'm surprised your fans can write."

> —Jerry Lawler, after Shawn Michaels
> thanked his fans for all their letters

"They're always being typecast as ignorant, but doctors and lawyers are watching us, the same way people in trailer parks do."

> —Mankind, *explaining how his book became a best-seller among the large audience of wrestling fans*

"How many of you out there would have the balls the size of grapefruits to slap your maker?"

> —Shane McMahon, *on overthrowing his dad as head of WWF*

"I wouldn't expect you to know, because amoebas don't feel very much."

> —Vince McMahon, *asking for sympathy from the fans*

"Everything that I do—everything that my family does—we do for you."

> —Vince McMahon, *describing his Bryan Adams–style love for his fans*

"I'm a billionaire. I can buy and sell every damn one of you in the arena tonight."

—*Vince McMahon*

"And the Pope was free."

—*Gene Okerlund, on more than 90,000 wrestling fans coming to Pontiac Silverdome, 5,000 more than came to see the Pope the following week*

"You are all unintelligent pieces of trailer-park trash."

—*The Rock, berating his fans during his days as a heel*

"You work your candy-asses off day after day nine to five for minimum wages."

—*The Rock, to his fans*

"What I'd like to have right now is for all of you fat, worthless, out-of-shape losers to shut your mouths for a minute so I can take my robe off."

—*Rick Rude, to his fans*

"All you are tobacco-chewing scumbag rednecks. You guys will always be losers."

—*Scott Steiner, to his fans*

"Most people are scumbags and they suck."

—*Scott Steiner, continuing to compliment his fan base*

"You have to face the facts that the vast majority of you are just born with inferior DNA."

—*Triple H, showing pride in his chemically influenced DNA*

"Thanks for the thousands in attendance, the millions at home, and goddamn it . . . let's get ready to suck it."

—*Triple H, reciting his motto*

"We come out here and put our lives on the line for you people each and every night, and you couldn't care less."

—*Triple H, feeling underappreciated*

HOWARD FINKEL

"If your last name was Finkel, would you name your kid Howard?"

—*Bobby Heenan*

"He's out of breath just cutting a promo."
—*Jerry Lawler, on Finkel, who had just challenged Road Dogg*

"The last time I saw something like that, I flushed it."
—*Jerry Lawler, on Finkel's unphotogenic appearance*

FIRING LINE

"McMahon 3:16 says, 'I've got the brass to fire your ass.'"

—*Vince McMahon, on his firing of Stone Cold Steve Austin*

"If you ever come into a WWF arena again, you'll have to buy a ticket."

> —*Vince McMahon, to Steve Austin after firing him*

RIC FLAIR

"I think Flair's recuperating in the La Brea Tar Pits with the rest of the fossils."

> —*Scott Hall, on the whereabouts*
> *of the ageless Flair*

"He keeps mouthing off about the wrestling tradition. Well, let me tell you about tradition: tradition bites."

> —*Scott Hall, on Ric Flair and the other*
> *elders of pro wrestling*

"When Ric Flair walks into the dressing room, all those boys making one million dollars a year should drop down and kiss his ass."

> —*Ricky Horton, on Ric Flair setting the stage for the*
> *glory that today's wrestlers receive*

"It was like the Yankees suing Mickey Mantle."
> —*Dave Meltzer,* Wrestling Observer *newsletter,*
> *on the WCW suing Ric Flair*

"The Mae West of pro wrestling."
> —*Roddy Piper, on Ric Flair's age*
> *and wrestling ability*

"Ric Flair was cool before it was hip to be cool."
> —*Bob Ryder, owner of 1Wrestling.com*

"I am sure he was something way back when."
> —*Scott Steiner, on Flair*

"You think a 50-year-old man is cool? I don't care how many times he says, 'Whooo.' "
> —*Scott Steiner, on Flair*

RIC FLAIR PHILOSOPHY

"To be that man, you've got to beat the man."

—*Ric Flair, his motto*

"Whether you love or hate me, you have to admit, I'm the best thing going."

—*Ric Flair*

"Diamonds are forever . . . so is Ric Flair."

—*Ric Flair*

MICK FOLEY

"A total toolshed."

—*Edge, on Foley. At least he's dealing with a full shed.*

"Most of the people I went to college with don't have their own action figures."

> —*Mick Foley, asked why he went into wrestling when he had a college education*

"If Mick ever had a thought, it'd die of loneliness."

> —*Jerry Lawler, on the intellectual prowess of Foley*

"You kvetch, you bitch, you cry, you moan—just like all the other people."

> —*Vince McMahon, admiring Foley's ability to use quiet determination in his bid for the belt*

"I didn't underestimate Steve Austin's abilities, I just overestimated yours."

> —*Vince McMahon, ever the coach with Foley, after Foley lost to Stone Cold Steve Austin*

MICK FOLEY PHILOSOPHY

"Everyone knows that Mick Foley takes a licking and keeps on ticking."

> —*Mick Foley, showing why he is a bestselling author*

"A man's got to know his limitations. That's pretty much my full-time job."

> —*Mick Foley, his philosophy as a pro wrestler (except that he has no limitations)*

FOOD FOR THOUGHT

"Anything raw and bloody—and hard to chew."

> —*Stone Cold Steve Austin, asked to name his favorite vegetarian food*

"You should see what we had for dinner."
> —*Hulk Hogan, after he, Diamond Dallas Page,*
> *and Goldberg went to a New York City*
> *restaurant and had huge steaks, lobsters,*
> *shrimp cocktails, and desserts*

"Nothing says lovin' like something from the oven."
> —*Mankind, after hitting Prince Al*
> *and Big Bossman with a tray*

"Let the Rock serve you up a nice big fat Rockburger
with some extra cheese."
> —*The Rock*

FOOTBALL

"You can't know the outcome of a match before it
happens and still call it a sport."
> —*Jamal Anderson, asked if pro*
> *wrestling was a sport*

"You would boo an Olympic champion and cheer Kurt Warner, a former arena football player who just happens to be on a lucky streak?"

> —*Kurt Angle, wrestling in St. Louis with Warner in attendance*

"Maybe if America were comprised of criminals, miscreants, and mediocre football players."

> —*Kurt Angle, slamming the Dallas Cowboys, often referred to as "America's Team"*

"Arrest those guys for imitating a football team."

> —*Jerry Lawler, after several Steelers players were seen at a WWF event during a difficult season*

"He probably thinks a quarterback is a refund."

> —*Jerry Lawler, guessing that Ken Shamrock knew nothing about football*

"Instead of going out and giving him a back-alley whipping like he deserves, I'm going to go to the ring and humiliate him."

> —*Steve McMichael, former NFL player, on wrestling Ric Flair, who allegedly had an affair with McMichael's wife*

"RJR Nabisco didn't call offering me the CEO job. Wrestling called."

> —*Steve McMichael, asked if he was embarrassed about going from the NFL to pro wrestling*

"I thought about bringing Bill in, but I found out they had a Big Mac Festival that day."

> —*Lawrence Taylor, asked if he was going to have Bill Parcells in his corner for a match with Bam Bam Bigelow*

"A lot of guys don't watch football. They watch wrestling instead."

> —*John Thorton, Tennessee Titans player, on his teammates' TV-viewing preferences*

FRIENDSHIP

"The more money you make, the better friends you are."
—*Terry Funk, on success in wrestling and in life*

"A friend in need is a pest."
—*Bobby Heenan*

"A friend is like a fish—three days later, they stink."
—*Bobby Heenan*

"Nothing good usually comes from friendships here in the WWF."
—*Jerry Lawler*

TERRY FUNK

"He has been around since Colonel Sanders was a private."

—*Jerry Lawler, working his way through the ranks of his friends in pro wrestling*

"He's been getting his butt kicked since Flipper was a minnow."

—*Jerry Lawler, who has been a tough guy for about the same length of time*

"I heard, when he was a kid, the Three Wise Men helped him with his homework."

—*Jerry Lawler, on Funk*

GANGREL

"How could you people sit here and denigrate me? You mean to tell me you would prefer to cheer for a man who looks like a vampire?"

—*Kurt Angle, on wrestling Gangrel*

"One at a time, please."

—*Jerry Lawler, to Gangrel, who was getting on the scale*

LILLIAN GARCIA

"Pretty women with a little bit of talent are a dime a dozen."

—*Vince McMahon, on threatening to fire Garcia as an announcer*

GOD BLESS THE USA

"This country would be completely devastated if my streak came to an end."

> —*Kurt Angle, on his undefeated streak*

"When the people vote for me, they're voting for America."

> —*Bob Backlund, running for Congress*

"Everything's fine now. Nobody will vote because everything's fine. As long as you got Cheetos, beer, and wrestling, we're fine."

> —*David Letterman, on the status of the United States before the 2000 election*

GODFATHER

"My image is tarnished just stepping into the ring with
a piece of crap like you."

—*Chris Jericho, to the Godfather (he wouldn't
dare say that to Marlon Brando)*

GODWINN BROTHERS

"I heard the Godwinns were at the mall and the power
went out, so they were stuck on the escalator for two
hours."

—*Jerry Lawler, on why the Godwinns
don't live in California*

"They're so southern, they're related to themselves."

—*Jerry Lawler, on the Godwinns*

"If these guys' brains were bacon, they would be
Sizzlean."

—*Jerry Lawler, king of the slam, on the Godwinns*

HENRY GODWINN

"Henry Godwinn has got so many missing teeth, it looks like his tongue is in jail."

—Jerry Lawler

"Henry Godwinn is the only guy I know who has a burglar alarm on his trash can."

—Jerry Lawler, complimenting the culinary tastes of Godwinn

PHINNEUS GODWINN

"When Phinneus gets those armpits around your nose, you will go out instantly."

—Jerry Lawler, on Godwinn's secret tactics

"Living proof of what happens when first cousins marry."

—Jim Ross, tracing Phinneus Godwinn's lineage

GOLDBERG

"Are these the friends I'd like Bill to bring to dinner?
I don't think so."

*—Ethel Goldberg, on her son
Bill's fellow WCW wrestlers*

"He's not a doctor, but I'll tell you something. He makes
ten times what a doctor makes."

*—Ethel Goldberg, on her son not
being a doctor like his dad*

"Underneath, Goldberg is about as savage as instant
pudding."

—Rick Reilly, Sports Illustrated *columnist*

GOLDBERG PHILOSOPHY

"If I was out here wearing a dress, painting my face up
like a clown . . . I'd rather dig a ditch."

—Goldberg, on the tactics of Dennis Rodman

"It's not in my repertoire."

—*Goldberg, on doing comedy routines*

"I'm an actor. Like Mel Gibson, I assume a character."

—*Goldberg, who isn't up for an Academy Award*

"Force equals mass times acceleration."

—*Goldberg, physicist*

GOLDUST

"Goldust put the fun in dysfunctional."

—*Jerry Lawler*

"You've got to believe that his family tree certainly needs trimming."

—*Jim Ross*

GORGEOUS GEORGE

"Like any other wrestler. Bad."

> —*Verne Gagne, asked how Gorgeous George smelled after his handlers sprayed perfume on George before he entered the ring*

BILLY GUNN

"They ought to call you Dumb Ass Billy Gunn."

> —*Stone Cold Steve Austin, creating a new nickname for Bad Ass Billy Gunn*

"Blondes have no fun. . . . They're just stupid."

> —*Eddie Guerrero, on Billy Gunn*

"It'll be the perfect ass versus the people's ass."

> —*Bad Ass Billy Gunn, on wrestling against the Rock. Now guess who is who.*

"It's Mr. Ass, the premier, the primo, the perfect ass."
> —Billy Gunn, not sure if he's insulting
> or complimenting himself

"You can kiss my royal ass."
> —Billy Gunn, taking the high road
> against an opponent

"You call yourself Mr. Ass. I call you Mr. Ass Kisser."
> —Mankind, to Billy Gunn

HAIL TO THE CHIEF

"I'd love to get him in the ring one more time before he becomes president."
> —Hulk Hogan, referring to Jesse Ventura

"I'm ten times more popular than Ventura."
> —Hulk Hogan, on the possibility of
> Ventura's running for president

"Put America first. Let's not worry about all the hungry people in other countries."

> —*Hulk Hogan, explaining the global strategy he would adopt if he were elected president*

"I saved my money, and I may find a penny or two lying around for the campaign. I need the write-offs anyway."

> —*Hulk Hogan, on how he would finance his presidential campaign*

"I was getting so popular, I told my wife I should run for president, but I didn't want to take a cut in pay."

> —*Hulk Hogan, who evidently has a different set of priorities than George W. Bush*

"Wherever he's going, I've already been."

> —*Hulk Hogan, on why he would be a better president than Bill Clinton*

"I thank the [fans] for sticking with me—and this helps me segue into being the next president of the United States."

> —*Hulk Hogan, preparing for his presidential debate*

"If he was president, the country's bird would be the middle finger."

> —*Jerry Lawler, on Stone Cold Steve Austin running for president*

"Wouldn't the president of the United States be anyone's role model?"

> —*Sunny, asked if Hillary Clinton was a role model while her husband was president*

"We talked about cigars. He's got a good collection in his office."

> —*Jesse Ventura, asked what he and President Clinton talked about when Ventura stayed overnight at the White House*

HAIR IT IS

"The Captain Lou Albano look."
> —*Brett Favre, on shaving his goatee*

"That's a nice haircut if you're going to the chair."
> —*Bobby Heenan, commenting on the*
> *Road Warrior's coiffure*

"Vader's gonna beat Hogan so hard, he [Hogan] will grow hair."
> —*Bobby Heenan, revealing what's really*
> *under Hogan's do-rag*

"Her goatee is thicker than his."
> —*Bobby Heenan, on Big Bossman's mother*

"Your head would get so big, your toupee wouldn't be able to fit on it."
> —*Jerry Lawler, explaining to Vince McMahon what*
> *would happen if Lawler were to praise McMahon*

"Your hair is looking better every day. It even has imitation dandruff."

—*Jerry Lawler, complimenting Vince McMahon's new hairstyle*

"Look, McMahon, there's some extra hair for your toupee."

—*Jerry Lawler, after Mankind ripped an opponent's hair out*

"Go back to Supercuts and get your five dollars back."

—*The Rock, on Big Show's brand-new hairdo*

SCOTT HALL

"I'm gonna kick ya where the Good Lord split ya."

—*Booker T, using free verse to describe what he would do to Hall*

"I'd like to fight him anywhere: the ring, the hallway, the parking lot, anywhere he wants."

—*Goldberg, on Hall*

STAN "THE MAN" HANSEN

"The Bad Man from Borger, Texas."

—*Anonymous, a general description of Hansen*

BRET HART

"I was the Robert De Niro of wrestling."

—*Bret Hart, defaming the great actor*

"If we in America can find it in our hearts to forgive Bill Clinton, we sure as heck can find it to forgive Bret Hart."

—*Rowdy Roddy Piper*

"There ain't much difference between Canadian white trash and American white trash."

—Scott Steiner, on Bret Hart,
who hails from Canada

HART FAMILY

"Ever since I heard of the Hart family tree, I wanted to chop it down."

—Jerry Lawler

OWEN HART

"Looks like Owen has opened up a can of haul-ass."

—Jerry Lawler, after Hart burned
rubber upon leaving the ring

STU HART

"Why don't you put your teeth in backwards and eat
  yourself."

> —*Jerry Lawler, referring to Hart's*
> *age and dental hygiene*

"Stu Hart is so old that when he was born, the Dead Sea
  was just sick."

> —*Jerry Lawler*

"I'm not saying that Stu Hart is old, but I hear Anna
  Nicole Smith is asking him out on a date."

> —*Jerry Lawler, on Hart and the*
> *infamous millionairess*

HARTFORD

"Call me a moving van so I can get the heck out of this town before I kill myself."

> *—Kurt Angle, on the quaintness of this New England city*

"Debra wouldn't be caught dead in a place like Hartford, Connecticut."

> *—Jeff Jarrett, on fans in Hartford screaming to see his valet, Debra*

"You idiot, this is Hartford."

> *—Jerry Lawler, after Mick Foley said he was glad to be back at Harvard*

MICHAEL HAYES

"Rock will knock your teeth so far down your throat,
you'll have to stick a toothbrush up your ass to brush
'em."

—The Rock, who does not suffer fools kindly

BOBBY HEENAN

"A pat on the back is only 12 inches from a kick in the
rear."

—Bobby Heenan, explaining office politics

"I had a guy give up one time during instruction."

*—Bobby Heenan, describing what a
great wrestler he was*

"I'm a legend in this sport. If you don't believe me, ask
me."

—Bobby Heenan

"If you keep quiet, no one will know how stupid you
   are."

MARK HENRY

"Mark Henry, you're nothing more than a big dumb
   Olympic failure."
                    *—Buh Buh Ray Dudley, admiring the skills
                    that made Henry an Olympian*

"You can take one look at Mark Henry and see that if
   he won a gold medal, he'd just take it and have it
   bronzed."
                    —Jerry Lawler

"I'm going to hit Mark Henry so hard, he's going to
   have to spend $14 to send me a postcard."
                    —Jerry Lawler

HILLBILLY JIM

"You're talking to a guy who thinks the bathroom should be outside 50 feet in back of the house."
—Bobby Heenan, on Hillbilly Jim

"The Hick from Mud Lick."
—Bobby Heenan, on Hillbilly Jim

"Don't go messin' with a country boy."
—Hillbilly Jim, on being 6'7", 300 pounds

HULK HOGAN

"The worst-kept secret in the world is that I hate Hollywood Hulk Hogan in life, in death."
—Ric Flair

"He's not pointing to anybody, he's showing how high he can count."

—Bobby Heenan, said when the Hulk was pointing to a fan

"I don't want to be part of any organization that Hulk Hogan is in charge of."

—Bobby Heenan

"Welcome back to the House that Hollywood Built."

—Hulk Hogan, on his comeback in the WCW

"My wife doesn't want me to quit, my kids don't want me to quit, the promoters don't want me to quit, the fans don't want me to quit, and the IRS really doesn't want me to quit."

—Hulk Hogan, contemplating retirement

"People know Hulk Hogan like they know McDonald's and Chevrolet."

—Hulk Hogan, an American institution

"The man who is a legend in this business has now become a parody of himself."

—*Chris Jericho*

"I feel sorry for Hulk. I hate picking on an old man."

—*Jay Leno*

"I don't know what it is, but I can't look at Hulk Hogan and believe that this is the end result of millions and millions of years of evolution."

—*Jim Murray*

"Where's Hogan, out doing another episode of 'Blunder in Paradise'?"

—*Kevin Nash, on Hogan's Academy Award–nominated role*

"A bald-headed reject from the glue factory."

—*Randy Savage, on Hogan*

"I come off like Deion Sanders in Hulk Hogan's body."

—*Shannon Sharpe, self-description*

"Obviously, the one vitamin he forgot to take was Rogaine."

—Scott Steiner, on Hulk's pate not matching his physique

"Maybe his wife wasn't telling him the truth or the mirrors in the house don't work."

—Scott Steiner

"The guy is 47 or 48 years old and he can't even walk to the ring straight. He limps to the ring."

—Scott Steiner, diagnosing the Hulk's problem

"You get tired of watching a guy like Hogan, who has got zero athletic ability left in him."

—Scott Steiner

"I think he's going to be remembered for the old pathetic piece of garbage he is right now."

—Scott Steiner, on the legacy of the world's most famous wrestler

"What's with the haircut? I mean, there's three people in the world [who look like that]—him, Bozo the Clown, and Ronald McDonald."

—*Scott Steiner, on Hogan's hairdo*

"Hulk Hogan. He's like a mountain with feet."
—*Judy Tenuta, comedienne, on her favorite actor*

"He's nothing but a Jesse wanna-be."
—*Jesse Ventura, responding to Hogan's vow to seek the presidency*

"He's copied me throughout his career."
—*Jesse Ventura, asked if he was surprised about Hogan's interest in a political career*

CRASH HOLLY

"Just because you lost the title, you can't get a girlfriend, and you still collect Beanie Babies, doesn't make you any less of a man."

> —Hardcore Holly, talking to his less macho cousin

"I'd be jealous, too, if my cousin was Saturday-morning cartoon superstar Elroy Jetson."

> —Chris Jericho, to Hardcore Holly
> about his cousin Crash

HOLLY FAMILY

"Set up two Holly pins, roll down this ramp, and score a 7–10 idiot split."

> —Chris Jericho, presenting his strategy for
> wrestling the terrible twosome

HARDCORE HOLLY

"I know I'm tough, because I'm hardcore 24/7."
>—*Hardcore Holly, his tough-guy philosophy*

"You can bring some cognac out for me and I'll bring some Rogaine out for you."
>—*Chris Jericho, to Hardcore*

"There ain't gonna be nothin' jolly about Bob Holly's Christmas."
>—*Chris Jericho, on wrestling Bob Holly just before Christmas*

"He would keep going to the pit stop to ask for directions."
>—*Jerry Lawler, on what would happen if Hardcore Holly followed his true love and became a race car driver*

HOOPS

"Rodzilla in the House."

—*Hulk Hogan, on being part of a*
tag team with Rodman

"You got a chance to hit a guy, you don't go to jail,
there's no lawsuit, and you get paid for it."

—*Karl Malone, on the benefits of pro*
wrestling over pro basketball

"I need you, Hulk. I need the Hulk out here."

—*Shaquille O'Neal, asking for Hulk Hogan's*
help after getting hacked repeatedly

"I'm Shaquille O'Neal. I don't need a backstage pass."

—*Shaquille O'Neal, after Vince McMahon*
asked him for a backstage pass

"Denise."

—*Diamond Dallas Page, on what he and*
most of America call Dennis Rodman

"I like it that guys get to talk trash and act on it. They get to kick ass."

> —*Dennis Rodman, on the three-ring circus that is wrestling and basketball*

HORSEMEN

"They pound on this Horseman any longer, he's going to the glue factory."

> —*Bobby Heenan, one of the Horsemen getting beat up in the WCW*

HOTELS

"I'm almost like a regular there."

> —*Stone Cold Steve Austin, after being banned from having breakfast at the Plaza for wearing shorts*

"Smackdown Hotel. It's on the corner of Know-Your-Role Boulevard and Jabroni Drive."

—The Rock, telling Mankind where the Rock is going to take him

CURTIS HUGHES

"He can scare a hot dog off a bun."

—Jerry Lawler, on Hughes's visage

HULKAMANIA PHILOSOPHY

"What ya gonna do when the 24-inch pythons run wild on you?"

—Hulk Hogan, his trademark phrase

"My God and my country and my Hulkamaniacs are gonna live forever."

—Hulk Hogan

"If I were a betting man, I wouldn't bet against Hulk Hogan, brother."

—Hulk Hogan

"The greater the gladiator is, the more enemies he has."
—Hulk Hogan, on how he sees his
role in professional wrestling

SIR OLIVER HUMPERDINK

"He looks like something that fell out of a deck of cards."

—Bobby Heenan, on the frilly Humperdink

IRON SHEIK

"To make scrap metal out of the Iron Sheik."
—Hulk Hogan, asked what his
goals were as a wrestler

JAIL TIME

"I once asked him what came at the end of the sentence and he said parole."
> —*Bobby Heenan, on a wrestler he talked to who had an extensive knowledge of the criminal justice system*

"Usually Mankind is on America's Most Unwanted list."
> —*Jerry Lawler, on Mankind, who was about to be arrested*

"Austin fought the law and the law won."
> —*Jerry Lawler, on Stone Cold Steve Austin's arrest*

JEFF JARRETT

"Let me introduce myself. My name is Jeff Jarrett, and I'm a man's man."
> —*Jeff Jarrett, his motto*

"Nobody ever said Jeff Jarrett was class valedictorian."
—*Jerry Lawler, on Jarrett not being the sharpest knife in the drawer*

CHRIS JERICHO

"You're the one coming out here every week, whining and crying like you've got a yeast infection."
—*Chyna, to Jericho, in response to Jericho saying she's not tough enough to be a pro wrestler*

"It's called Chyna envy."
—*Chyna, on the constant battles between Chyna and Jericho*

"He was worried that a woman would steal his glory—which, of course, I did."
—*Chyna, after laying Jericho down in a match*

"You were destroyed by the toughest and meanest man in the WWF."

—Chris Jericho, to Curtis Hughes,
whom he had just defeated

"You can't handle Y2J, because I am one bad mamma jamma."

—Chris Jericho

"I know she's got a sexual crush on Y2J. And with a gorgeous face like this, can you blame her?"

—Chris Jericho, referring to Chyna

"You wanna talk about doggy style? Well, tonight, prepare to be destroyed by Ayatollah style."

—Chris Jericho, facing the Road Dogg
in a battle of the biggest bite

"Jericho was in another time zone."

—Jim Ross, after Big Show threw Chris Jericho

"Great big piece of cheese to draw some rat."
>
> —*Triple H, trying to entice Chris Jericho*
> *to wrestle him*

CHRIS JERICHO PHILOSOPHY

"No one is going to remember Y2K, because all they're going to be talking about is Y2J."
>
> —*Chris Jericho, said as the year 2000 began*

"The Ayatollah of Rock and Rollah."
>
> —*Chris Jericho, his fear-inducing nickname*

JOB PERFORMANCE

"If you're not born in the business, it's hard to grasp."
>
> —*The Rock, whose father was a pro wrestler*

"Steve Austin will never be employee of the month."
—*Jim Ross, after Austin hit Vince McMahon*

AHMED JOHNSON

"Ahmed Johnson's got an IQ of two, and it takes three just to grunt."
—*Jerry Lawler*

"If stupidity was water, Ahmed Johnson would be Niagara Falls."
—*Jerry Lawler*

JUNKYARD DOG

"His parents had nine months, and the best they could come up with is Junkyard."
—*Bobby Heenan, on Junkyard Dog's underdeveloped state*

SID JUSTICE

"He may be the dumbest big man I've ever met."
—*Jake Roberts, on Justice*

"Sid believes that the meek shall inherit the earth. But only after I'm through with it."
—*Jake Roberts*

KANE

"You can bet your ass Stone Cold Steve Austin is gonna bring all the marshmallows, all the hot dogs, all the beer."
—*Stone Cold Steve Austin, after Kane said he would set himself on fire if he lost to Austin*

"The sensitive side's overrated."
—*Kane, on being called cuddly*

"Brimstone Breath."

—Jerry Lawler, on Kane's oral hygiene

"He flipped Viscera like a cheese omelet."

—Jerry Lawler, on Kane

"I wish we could get him to go back in."

*—Jerry Lawler, on X-Pac helping to
get Kane out of his shell*

"If you put Kane's brain in a bird, it would fly
backwards."

—The Rock

ANDY KAUFMAN

"Andy Kaufman's mom wanted a girl, his father wanted
a boy, and they were both satisfied."

*—Jerry Lawler, on the infamous comic
and wrestler of women (and men)*

BILLY KIDMAN

"He couldn't sell out the flea market on its best day."
—*Hulk Hogan, on the charisma*
and charm of Kidman

KONNAN

"He couldn't draw money if you dipped him in glue and dragged him through Fort Knox."
—*Jim Cornette, on Konnan's popularity*

KILLER KOWALSKI

"No other wrestler has ever been more intimidating than the Killer."
—*Lou Albano*

JERRY LAWLER

"There's nothing wrong with being naked. I was born that way."

—*Jerry Lawler*

"I can talk a good fight and I can fight a good fight."
—*Jerry Lawler, on his skills both in and out of the ring*

"The only thing worse than edible panties is edible Depends."

—*Jerry Lawler, on aging female wrestlers*

"Manure happens."

—*Jerry Lawler, his general philosophy*

"I'm not superstitious, because I know that's unlucky."
—*Jerry Lawler*

"Your sycophantic reveler, with your fancy clothes and your middle-class suburbia."

—*The Raven, on Lawler*

LEGAL EAGLES

"If you want to talk legal, drive 35 miles per hour."

—*Bobby Heenan, stressing the importance of being a law-abiding citizen*

"You have the team of attorneys that you have work so diligently at scaring everybody under the sun."

—*Triple H, on not being intimidated by McMahon and his legal team*

"If lawyers can run, why can't wrestlers? We certainly have enough lawyers."

—*Jesse Ventura, on wrestlers running for political office*

LEGION OF DOOM

"They're not like wine. They get worse when they age."
—*Jerry Lawler, on the Legion of Doom*

"The older they get, the better they were."
—*Jerry Lawler*

"They have been written off more times than a business lunch, but they keep coming back."
—*Jim Ross*

JAY LENO

"This is serious business, joke man."
—*Hulk Hogan, talking about wrestling to Jay Leno*

"Jay is ready to prove that he can deliver the punches along with the punch lines."

—Alan Sharpe, publicist for the WCW,
on Leno wrestling in a WCW match

LET IT BLEED

"You want my blood—hell, I've got a truckload of it."

—Stone Cold Steve Austin, to the Undertaker,
who threatened to destroy Austin

"It will not be the first time, and it sure as hell will not be the last, because I've got an awful lot of blood to give."

—Mankind, on Triple H saying
he will make Mankind bleed

LOOKS COULD KILL

"Got the body that women love and men envy."
—*Lou Albano, appraising his own body*

"Never get into a fight with an ugly guy, because he's got nothing to lose."
—*Jerry Lawler*

"Is that your face, or did your neck throw up?"
—*Jerry Lawler, to a fan*

JOSE LOTHARIO

"Jose Lothario is so old, he has an autographed copy of the Bible."
—*Jerry Lawler*

LEX LUGER

"I like Lex Luger so much, I'd like to bash him in the side of his head with a chair."

—*Kevin Nash*

MABEL

"Mabel is so huge, when he was a baby, he probably got baptized at Sea World."

—*Jerry Lawler*

"He is not too nice if you disturb him during feeding time."

—*Jerry Lawler*

MARK MADDEN

"The best-looking man on television."

—*Mark Madden, former WCW announcer,*
describing himself

DEAN MALENKO

"Bore-us Malenko."

—*Chris Jericho, on Malenko's father's name*

MANKIND

"Everybody hates you. All the people at home—all these people in the arena hate you. And most importantly, Y2J hates you."

—*Chris Jericho, to Mankind*

"He's had more concussions than Elizabeth Taylor has had husbands."

—*Jerry Lawler, on Mankind*

"Mankind's got the future of an ice cube."

—*Jerry Lawler*

"He has fallen so far down the corporate ladder, he has splinters in his butt."

—*Jerry Lawler, on Mankind's fall from grace*

"I heard when he was born, his old man went down to the zoo and threw rocks at the stork."

—*Jerry Lawler*

"He's like one of those idiot savants—only without the savant part."

—*Jerry Lawler*

"Of all the things he's lost, I think he misses his mind the most."

—*Jerry Lawler*

"He is a few peas short of a casserole."

—Jerry Lawler

"A $400 suit on Mankind would look like socks on a rooster."

—Jerry Lawler

"He's not too smart, but he leads the league in nose hairs."

—Jerry Lawler, proving that everyone is good in at least one thing

"He looks like an unmade bed."

—Jerry Lawler

"The Halloween pumpkins on my front porch have more teeth than Mankind."

—Jerry Lawler

"I don't care what it is, I just worry about where it's been."

—Jerry Lawler, on Mr. Socko, Mankind's trusty prop

"If he were just a little smarter, he'd realize how stupid he was."

—Jerry Lawler, pointing out
Mankind's shortcomings

"I made your son Shane cry like a two-year-old with a poop in his pants."

—Mankind, to Vince McMahon

"You can't shine ca-ca."

—Vince McMahon, on attempts to
make Mankind look better

"You're nothing but a disillusioned, decrepit, disfigured monster."

—Vince McMahon, learning to use
all his d words in one sentence

"I hate people like you who rely on pillars of strength like me just to get through the day."

—Vince McMahon, to Mankind, who was
begging for a championship bout

"Rock's fans wanna see your fat cellulite ass go one-on-one with the Great One."

> —*The Rock, begging for a match with Mankind*

"I'm sorry, Mankind is not available. He is busy getting his ass kicked by the Great One."

> —*The Rock, taking messages for Mankind*

"I'm gonna knock the yellow off your teeth and slap the teeth out of your mouth."

> —*The Rock, to Mankind*

"It looks like a big monkey came out here and took a crap and out came Mankind."

> —*The Rock, explaining the theory of evolution*

MANKIND PHILOSOPHY

"Mankind is an entertaining son of a gun. Mankind is a pretty damn good author and is one hell of a fighter."

> —*Mankind, his own biggest fan*

"Know your mouth and shut your role."
>—*Mankind, parodying the Rock's "Know your role and shut your mouth"*

"It takes a good man to beat me, it just doesn't take him very long."
>—*Mankind, the underdog*

"The world's most polite wrestler."
>—*Mankind, on his own legacy*

MARRIAGE

"I now pronounce you as the unholy union of darkness."
>—*Paul Bearer, on the moving, emotional attempted wedding of the Undertaker to Stephanie McMahon*

"I'm not a doctor, but it seems like it would be a physical impossibility for you to produce an heir, seeing as your husband has absolutely no testicles."

—*Cactus Jack, to Stephanie McMahon about her husband, Triple H*

"I know all about cheating. I've had six very successful marriages."

—*Bobby Heenan, warning a wrestler not to cheat on his girlfriend*

"My first wife and I were happy for 20 years—then we met."

—*Jerry Lawler, on peeling the scales off his eyes*

"I got married by a judge. I should have asked for a jury."

—*Jerry Lawler*

"If I was a girl, I'd marry me, but Triple H would be a close second."

—*Jerry Lawler, who is obviously a little confused*

"Love your husband, honor your husband, but get as much as you can in your name."

> —*Jerry Lawler, advice to a pregnant woman*

"The only move you'll be doing is walking away from my husband."

> —*Stephanie McMahon, to Trish Stratus,*
> *who was flirting with Triple H*

MCMAHON'S BEST FRIEND

"McMahon thinks Snoop Doggy Dog belongs to Charlie Brown."

> —*Jerry Lawler*

MCMAHON'S GANG

"It doesn't even qualify as the Three Stooges—it's so pathetic, it's the Three Jackasses."

> —*Stone Cold Steve Austin, on McMahon and his cronies, Jerry Brisco and Pat Patterson*

SHANE MCMAHON

"A sniveling, little silver-spoon-sucking sissy."

> —*Mankind, on Shane McMahon receiving special treatment for being Daddy's little boy*

"Don't have enough sugar in that sack of testicles."

> —*The Rock, on McMahon's wimpiness*

"This kid needs an ass-whipping."

> —*Jim Ross, on the proper parenting techniques for Shane*

"You couldn't beat my ass if the other half was helping you."

—Test, taunting Shane

STEPHANIE MCMAHON

"I really admire you, kinda the way the people admire me for my Olympic gold medals."

—Kurt Angle, to someone he loves
almost as much as himself

"Evil shouldn't look that good, but I think she is evil."

—Jerry Lawler

VINCE MCMAHON

"It should be Jackass of the Year."

*—Stone Cold Steve Austin, on Vince McMahon
receiving a Humanitarian
of the Year Award*

"McMahon, don't you ever call me collect again, or I'll whoop your ass."

—Stone Cold Steve Austin, to Vince

"To me Vince McMahon is a genius for what he's done with wrestling. Baseball needs to do that."

*—Jose Canseco. (Time for a Cal Ripken–
Undertaker death match?)*

"I've got a sore hand, but I figure he's a lot sorer."

—Bret Hart, after a confrontation with McMahon

"You're so cheap, you won't even tip a canoe."

*—Jerry Lawler, to McMahon, referring
to his less-than-generous spirit*

"The most ruthless human being to ever walk the planet."

—Shane McMahon, on his dad

"You better get your attitude out of my face, before I slap the wrinkles out of yours."

—Shane McMahon, to his dad—
said respectfully, of course

"He will do almost anything or allow almost anything to be said, so long as the audience increases."

—David Nyhan, columnist for
the Boston Globe, *on Vince*

"That might be the only thing that's real."

—Burt Sugar, on the dislike Vince McMahon
and Ted Turner have for each other

"It's time you get your pencil-neck-geeked ass out here to face the reaper."

—The Undertaker, failing to notice that Vince
had started pumping iron

"You make a living on manipulating minds weaker than yours."

—The Undertaker, on Vince McMahon, pointing out the obvious while dissing the fans

"Darwin proved there was a theory of evolution. McMahon has taken us back to where we started."

—Baron Von Raschke

MEAN GENE

"Gene, do me a favor: go out and get a nice warm cup of shut-the-hell-up."

—Brian Adams, to Gene Okerlund on a cold day

"He could stand out there with a mannequin and get an interview out of him."

—David Penzer, ring announcer, on Mean Gene Okerlund

MEN'S WORLD

"They accepted me once I learned how to burp the alphabet."

—*Chyna*

"Women will never be the same as men until they can walk down the street with a bald head and a beer gut and still think they're beautiful."

—*Jerry Lawler, on the gender gap*

"It's only because the so-called men knew I could kick their ass."

—*Moolah, asked how she felt about not being able to wrestle men until recently*

SHAWN MICHAELS

"Shawn Michaels's ego is so big, he has his own zip code."

—Jerry Lawler, who has his own state

"He is never on vacation, 'cause he is on a permanent ego trip."

—Jerry Lawler, on Michaels

"You are one of the great WWF superstars of all time— there is no doubt about that—but as a commissioner, you suck."

—Vince McMahon, to Michaels, during Michaels's time as WWF commissioner

SHAWN MICHAELS PHILOSOPHY

"Of course I love you. Not as much as you love me, not as much as I love me."

> —*Shawn Michaels, to his wife Sherri during their breakup*

"The Heart Break Kid lies down for no one."

> —*Shawn Michaels*

"I'll bring the pain—all you need to do is show up."

> —*Shawn Michaels, telling an opponent what to expect*

"How does someone that looks this good hurt so bad?"

> —*Shawn Michaels, on himself, displaying his sensitive side*

"I'm the icon, the main event, the showstopper."

> —*Shawn Michaels*

MINNEAPOLIS

"The pig farm capital of the world."
—*Eric Bischoff, on Minneapolis*

"Very dreary and highly unimpressive."
—*William Regal, passing his royal judgment on Minneapolis*

MISS KITTY

"I am the class and dignity champion. And all that Miss Kitty does to this title is wipe her smut all over it."
—*Ivory, obviously a class act*

MR. FUJI

"He had the kind of smile you associate with a man who had just tossed Mr. Rogers into a tankful of piranhas."

—Tony Kornheiser, on Fuji

MR. PERFECT

"I am perfect."

—Mr. Perfect, his self-description in a nutshell

MONEY MACHINE

"I got enough money to last the rest of my life—if I live till tomorrow."

—Lou Albano, explaining how living frugally has paid off for him

"The worse you hurt each other, the more money you make."

—*Terry Funk, on wrestling bonuses*

"Professional wrestling—it's just a long cruel money trench, a plastic hallway filled with pimps and thieves."
—*Bret Hart, explaining why wrestling rocks*

"The money's the same whether you earn it or scam it."
—*Bobby Heenan, explaining why everyone should follow the path of virtue*

"I buy an ounce of gold every week. My CPA told me to."

—*Junkyard Dog*

"There's nothing wrong with making money. That's the American way."

—*Lex Luger*

"The only reason I haven't fired Stone Cold Steve Austin yet is because he makes me richer."

—*Vince McMahon*

GORILLA MONSOON

"I got a bunch of bananas in the back, and I know where you can stick every one of them."

—*Stone Cold Steve Austin, to Gorilla Monsoon*

"You call yourself a gorilla, but you come out here and hee-haw like a jackass."

—*Stone Cold Steve Austin*

"That tree-climbing, banana-eating fool."

—*Jim Cornette, on Gorilla Monsoon*

"Keep it up and I'm gonna knock you out."

—*Gorilla Monsoon, to Bobby Heenan*

MOVIE TIME

"Giving this movie a bad review is like hanging a 'Do Not Swim' sign over a toxic waste dump."
—Atlanta Constitution, *on* Ready to Rumble

"If I had his movie career, I wouldn't want any movie career."
—*Big Poppa Pump, on the Hulkster's unsuccessful movie career*

"He's got the *Something About Mary* thing going there."
—*Jerry Lawler, on Chris Jericho's hair sticking up*

"The problem with Hollywood is making sure we don't get involved with schlock."
—*Vince McMahon, on the Hollywood/wrestling connection and making sure that wrestling maintains its dignity*

"Austin's seen too many Oliver Stone movies."

*—Vince McMahon, on Stone Cold Steve Austin
complaining there was a conspiracy
against him*

"I'm here to chew bubble gum and kick ass. And I'm out of bubble gum."

—Rowdy Roddy Piper, one of his lines from They
Live, *a movie destined to be a classic*

"Next thing you know, they'll be telling me WWF wrestling is fake, too."

*—Jack Tunney, former WWF commissioner, after
expressing a desire to hold a wrestling match
in Jurassic Park and being told it was a
fictitious movie setting*

MUSIC TO MY EARS

" 'Take Me Out to the Ballgame' would be replaced by
Nine Inch Nails' Greatest Hits."

> —*Jim Caple,* USA Today *reporter, imagining if
baseball were owned by the WWF*

"He really shouldn't give up his day job."

> —*Edge, on the Rock singing "Smackdown Hotel"*

"I hope that when I am that age I'm enjoying the same
kind of success on my comeback tour."

> —*Ric Flair, after going to the Rolling
Stones' Reunion Tour*

"Grown men in skirts playing vacuum cleaners."

> —*Bobby Heenan, on bagpipe players,
a tradition he loves*

"There are two kinds of music I don't like—country and
western."

> —*Bobby Heenan*

"The Gloved One is in a lot of trouble. I'm gonna body-slam him out of the music industry just like I body-slammed Andre the Giant."

—*Hulk Hogan, on his music career and Michael Jackson*

"Then he won't win many matches."

—*Jerry Lawler, after Vince McMahon said that Road Dogg sings as well as he wrestles*

"I can sing a tune or two, but otherwise I suck."

—*The Rock*

KEVIN NASH

"Big Slimy."

—*Curt Hennig, revising Nash's nickname—Big Sexy*

"I just watched my gang find Hollywood Hogan, who ran out the back door, 'cause Hollywood knows he wants no part of Big Sexy."
—*Kevin Nash, displaying respect for his elders*

"Big Sexy in da house."
—*Kevin Nash, showing how many sentences in which he can use the words "Big Sexy"*

NEW AGE OUTLAWS

"I've got thirteen words for you. How much wood could a woodchuck chuck if a woodchuck could chuck wood?"
—*Bobby Heenan, asking the New Age Outlaws the ultimate unanswered question*

NEW WORLD ORDER

"Not one of those guys could launder his jockstrap."
—*Jim Cornette, on the New World Order making fun of Arn Anderson's retirement speech*

NEW YORK CITY

"We all know that if we wait for Patrick Ewing and the New York Knicks to bring home a title, we'd probably be waiting forever."

—*Kurt Angle, on his love of the New York sports scene*

"It's nice to be back in the city that Hollywood built."
—*Hollywood Hogan, at the New York Stock Exchange*

NORMAN

"Norman is so stupid, mind readers charge him half price."

—*Jim Cornette*

"You've heard of a picture worth a thousand words. That picture is worth a dose of Pepto-Bismol."

—*Jim Cornette, on a picture of Norman displayed at the Metropolitan Museum of Art*

O CANADA

"I used to think the only good thing that came out of Canada was maple syrup and Michael J. Fox. I was wrong, and I'm not wrong very often."

—*Kurt Angle, on his friends Edge and Christian, the Canadian tag team*

"I've won more golds in the past year than all the Canadians in the Olympic Games."

—*Kurt Angle, challenging our friends to the north*

"I'm from the City of Champions, and I'm going to give you a good Northern Atlantic ass-kickin'."

—*Chris Benoit, trying to get a rise out of Chris Jericho*

"Inbreds north of the border."

—*Eddie Guerrero, on his view of Canadians*

"It must be something in the Canadian beer that makes you want to become a wrestler, makes you grow your hair long."

—*Chris Jericho, explaining why Canadian wrestlers are so wild*

"Most of them look like him—or at least most of the women."

—*Jerry Lawler, on Mankind relating well to the Canadian fans*

"Does Canada even have an army? Our Salvation Army could kick their army's butt."

—*Jerry Lawler*

"I would rather play Naked Twister with the Golden Girls than live in Canada."

—*Jerry Lawler*

OLD DAYS

"There used to be a lot of camaraderie in the business, but no more. Now you've got to cut throats."

—*Jake Roberts*

"My only gimmick's my boots and tights."

—*Bruno Sammartino, on the way things used to be*

ONE MAN GANG

"He's good to have at picnics—he keeps the flies off the food."

> —*Bobby Heenan, on One Man Gang*

OPPONENTS

"It was an honor just being in the ring with you."

> —*Kurt Angle, what he expects his opponent to say after losing*

"If you want me to beat his sorry little ass all over this arena, give me a 'Hell, yeah.'"

> —*Stone Cold Steve Austin, offering a rallying cry that incites rabid fan participation*

DIAMOND DALLAS PAGE

"You love me, you hate me, you'll never forget me."
—*Diamond Dallas Page, spewing forth*
his modest motto

"Diamond Dallas Page, when I look at you, I see white trash. When I look at the people in the crowd, I see white trash. So maybe you are the people's champion."
—*Scott Steiner, on Diamond Dallas Page*
claiming to be the people's champion

PAIN

"I would rather hurt a man than love a woman."
—*Cactus Jack*

"Waking up without pain."
—*Mankind, asked what he appreciates*
most on any given day

"Painus in Uranus."

> —*The Rock, on what he would do to an opponent in astrological terms*

"We traded a lot of blows, brother. A lot of aches and pain."

> —*Jimmy Snuka, on his matches against Rowdy Roddy Piper and Don Muraco*

ROWDY RODDY PIPER

"I heard a rumor that his mom and dad ran away from home."

> —*Bobby Heenan, on the reaction of Rowdy's parents when Rowdy was born*

"He certainly is unfit to wear a skirt."

> —*Gloria Steinem, on the kilts of Rowdy Roddy Piper*

ROWDY RODDY PIPER PHILOSOPHY

"I'm so fast I can spit in the wind, duck, and let it hit
  that old lady behind me."
>   —*Rowdy Roddy Piper, respecting his elders*

"Just when you think you know the answers, I change
  the question."
>   —*Rowdy Roddy Piper, a psychic sidestepper*

"Real men wear kilts."
>   —*Rowdy Roddy Piper, proclaiming his manhood*

PLAYBOY

"Basically, the truth is I want to get naked."
>   —*Chyna, on why she was appearing
>   naked in* Playboy

"I don't do what Rock does and I couldn't do what Rock does, but then he couldn't pose nude for *Playboy*, could he?"

—*Chyna*

"I'm not saying that they're not beautiful, but I could cut their little peppered bones for breakfast."
—*Chyna, on playmates in* Playboy

"To be the best governor I can be, to continue being devoted to my family, and to not do *Playboy* interviews."
—*Jesse Ventura, his resolutions for 2001*

POLICE

"A lot of cops are wrestling fans. They usually let me slide."

—*Stone Cold Steve Austin, on not getting a ticket for speeding*

"You have the right to suffer. You have the right to feel pain. If you wish to have an attorney present, I'll hurt him too."

>—Big Bossman, said while wearing a police uniform

POLITICS

"Our governor can beat up your governor."

>—Anonymous, on Jesse Ventura becoming Minnesota governor

"A vote for Jesse Ventura is a vote for Jesse Ventura."

>—Popular slogan in Minnesota gubernatorial election

"Both wrestling and politics are full-contact sports."

>—Bob Backlund, on running for Congress

"When people see you in tights every Saturday, they really know you."

—John DeFazio, member of city council
in Pennsylvania and a pro wrestler
on weekends

"Last Congress, the House of Representatives was run with the dignity of the World Wide Wrestling Federation."

—Dick Gephardt, House Minority Leader,
on the 1999 Congress Smackdown

"I don't remember Walter Cronkite asking Haystacks Calhoun how he felt about Richard Nixon's wage and price guidelines."

—Jay Leno, on Larry King asking
Hulk Hogan about politics

"Americans know they can trust an entertainer as politician more than a politician as entertainer."
—Vince McMahon, Mr. Trustworthy himself

"Sorry you didn't get the WWF Smackdown."
> —*Karl Rove, George W. Bush's strategist, on the tame debate between vice-presidential candidates Dick Cheney and Joe Lieberman*

"Maybe my years in pro wrestling, doing all those interviews, helped me to debate and be quick on my feet."
> —*Jesse Ventura*

"Taking it out in the ring against hails of insults—what better training is there for public office?"
> —*Jesse Ventura, on endorsing Kane for president*

"I'm beginning to kind of like this gig."
> —*Jesse Ventura, confusing his role as governor with the band he fronted in the 1960s*

"The Three Stooges . . . Their eyes follow you around the room."
> —*Jesse Ventura, upon first entering the Governor's Office, which had pictures of three former governors hanging on the wall*

"Wrestling isn't that different from politics. Both can be somewhat dirty."

—*Jesse Ventura, stating the obvious*

"Keep it simple and stupid."

—*Jesse Ventura, his political philosophy*

"Politics is way more cutthroat than wrestling."

—*Jesse Ventura, stating the obvious*

PRINCE ALBERT

"This guy has to comb his wrist to see what time it is."

—*Jerry Lawler*

SCOTT PUTSKI

"This kid is so dumb, he stayed up all night studying for a urine test."

—*Jim Cornette, on Putski*

"Obi-Wan Jabronie."

—*Kanyon, giving Putski a new nickname*

RAVEN

"You greasy-haired little freak."

—*Bob Holly, referring to the Raven's hip hairstyle*

"Once again, the flock has let me down."

—*Raven, after his partners lost a match*

RAVEN PHILOSOPHY

"The world is full of kings and queens, who will blind
your eyes and steal your dreams."

—Raven

"As the path grows brighter, it also grows darker, and I
will be your guide down agony's bleak path."

—Raven, in the spirit of Edgar Allan Poe

REFS

"You need experience, the ability to be respected in the
ring, and good health insurance."

*—Randy "Pee Wee" Anderson, on the
qualifications for being a ref*

"I think Pat Patterson refereed the match between David
and Goliath."

*—Jerry Lawler, on Patterson's long
experience in the ring*

"That ref couldn't see an elephant in a telephone booth."

—Jerry Lawler, on a ref with peripheral vision difficulties

"These new refs are worse than the old ones—if that's possible."

—Jerry Lawler, after the old refs went on strike

"Will you officiate this matchup in the time-honored tradition of WWF referees?"

—Vince McMahon, to a ref before a title match, essentially asking the ref if he'd look the other way

"As long as you are in this state, you hold no power here. The Body rules."

—Jesse Ventura, to Vince McMahon, on Ventura wanting to referee a WWF match while he was governor

"I'm not going to stop having fun. My critics didn't vote for me anyway."

> —*Jesse Ventura, on being criticized for being a WWF ref after being elected Minnesota governor*

WILLIAM REGAL

"Roll up your candy bum."

> —*The Rock, on Regal, who is English, making British people roll their eyes*

"You are nothing more than a suit-wearing, bug-eyed, cockamamie punk-ass."

> —*The Rock, to his British rival*

RELIGION

"You read your Psalms and talk about John 3:16—well,
Austin 3:16 says I just whooped your ass."
> —*Stone Cold Steve Austin, misinterpreting the Bible*

"I gave that up for Lent."
> —*Mankind, after the Rock said Mankind*
> *could kiss his butt*

RETIREMENT

"I'll put my guns in the ground. I can't shoot them
anymore."
> —*Bret Hart, announcing his retirement*
> *Bob Dylan–style*

"When it's over, it's over. I ain't waiting around."
> —*Jake Roberts, on retirement*

"Bam, Bam, I hope you don't like your job."

> —Lawrence Taylor, warning Bam Bam Bigelow
> he will have to retire after wrestling LT

DUSTY RHODES

"I feel like I'm doing a pay-per-view with Inspector Clouseau."

> —Bobby Heenan, on working with Dusty Rhodes

STEVE RICHARDS

"You will never have the talent or the charisma of Y2J, so get out of here, jerky."

> —Chris Jericho, to Richards

"Everybody knows that your Stevie Bear is not a fighter, he's a lover."

> —Steve "Elvis" Richards

WENDI RICHTER

"A hundred and fifty pounds of twisted steel and sex appeal."

—Wendi Richter, self-description

RIKISHI

"You've got enough ass right there to make a total eclipse of the sun."

—Hardcore Holly, to Rikishi

"He qualifies for group insurance all by himself."

—Jerry Lawler, on the mass of human flesh that is Rikishi

"The guy's like a pimple on prom night. He keeps popping up."

—Jerry Lawler, on Rikishi's ability to fight back

"His belly button doesn't have lint—it has sweaters."

—*Jerry Lawler*

"You think they've got a room big enough for Rikishi at the Smackdown Hotel?"

—*Jerry Lawler, on the Rock wrestling Rikishi*

"You can actually park a small car in the dimples of his rear end."

—*Jerry Lawler*

"If his butt starts beeping, that means he's backing up."

—*Jerry Lawler*

"If you told him to haul ass, it would take two trips."

—*Jerry Lawler*

"His rear end kinda looks like the moon from about three miles out."

—*Jerry Lawler*

"I think Macy's wants him to be a float in next year's parade."

—*Jerry Lawler*

"If he bends over, you can show two movies on his butt."

—*Jerry Lawler*

"A thong-wearing fatty."

—*The Rock*

"You are gonna get, literally, the single biggest ass-kicking of a lifetime."

—*The Rock, to Rikishi*

"Bring your fat, cellulite-infested, stinkin' carcass down to this ring."

—*Val Venis, after noting how Rikishi had begun working out more consistently*

ROAD DOGG

"Road Dogg is fixing to be roadkill, if he knows what I'm talking about."

—*Hardcore Holly, on wrestling Road Dogg*

"He was the first soldier over there to get shot at by both sides."

—*Jerry Lawler, on Road Dogg serving in Desert Storm*

"He's not a road dog, he's a hot dog. Put some mustard on him."

—*Jerry Lawler*

"I don't believe he's got a crushed disk. You've got to have a spine to have a crushed disk."

—*Jerry Lawler, on Road Dogg's whimpering in pain and complaining of having a crushed disk*

"I bet he wishes he knew the number for Dial-A-Prayer."
—*Jerry Lawler, while Kane was throwing around Road Dogg*

"A blemish in the Rock's buttocks."
—*The Rock, on Road Dogg*

"That's real creative, real innovative, saying the same thing night in and night out. Be like the Rock. Be electrifying."
—*The Rock, making fun of Road Dogg's stage mike time*

ROAD DOGG PHILOSOPHY

"Welcome to the Dogg-house."
—*Road Dogg, his catchphrase*

"Welcome to my Dogg-house, where we do it all the time doggy style."

—*Road Dogg, quoting from his philosophical manifesto*

ROAD TRIP

"This town has nothing going for it right now. . . . I'm the only thing left in these people's lives."

—*Kurt Angle, on Pittsburgh*

"Virginia is for lovers—provided those lovers are not from the same family."

—*Kurt Angle*

"Speaking of sore losers, how fitting is it that we're in the capital city of sore losers: Buffalo, New York."

—*Kurt Angle, during a visit to Buffalo*

"The greatest thing to come out of here—the Islanders and Billy Joel—haven't been any good since 1983."

—*Kurt Angle, on Long Island*

"We all know how easy it is to catch something contagious in this town."

—*Kurt Angle, at a match in Rochester, New York, explaining why Stephanie McMahon was not at the event*

"Like so many other cities in this nation, Chicago—you have a serious case of the uglies."

—*Edge and Christian, who are from Canada*

"It must be nice to actually have some winners within your state boundaries."

—*Edge and Christian, during a match in Phoenix, Arizona, after which they were run out of town*

"Parts unknown usually means downtown Newark."

—*Bobby Heenan*

"Do you want to know why it's the heartland of America? Because there is no brain."

> —*Jerry Lawler, on Nebraska wrestling fans*

"If your mom and dad got a divorce, would they still be brother and sister?"

> —*Jerry Lawler, to fans from Alabama*

"That's southern hospitality for you."

> —*Vince McMahon, after being called a derogatory name in Kentucky*

"Rocklanta."

> —*The Rock, on what the city of Atlanta should be called. For some reason, he did not receive a key to the city.*

"The Show Me State of St. Louis, Missouri."

> —*Scott Steiner, a bit off on his geography*

ROAD WARRIOR HAWK

"When you're all done yappin', it's time for some open-
   hand slappin'."

—Road Warrior Hawk

JAKE ROBERTS

"Five million people watching RAW, and Jake is not one
   of them."

—Jerry Lawler, on Roberts's laying
facedown on the mat

"Jake the Snake's two best friends are Jim Beam and
   Jack Daniel's."

—Jerry Lawler

"I just got a note from a doctor saying that there was a
   possible trace of blood in Jake the Snake's alcohol
   stream."

—Jerry Lawler

ROCK

"GQ, smooth-talking, smart aleck."

—Kurt Angle, dissing the Rock

"I'm gonna walk right into the Smackdown Hotel, check into room 3:16, and beat the SOB."

—Stone Cold Steve Austin

"Little poor man's Elvis imitation."

—Stone Cold Steve Austin, on the not-so-poor-any-longer-now-that-he's-a-movie-star Rock

"Don't give me none of your silly nursery rhymes, Rock."

—Stone Cold Steve Austin, on the Rock's mike time

"The People's Joke."

—Chris Benoit, on the Rock

"I smell something, but I still think it might be Rock's big cellulite ass."

—*Jerry Lawler*

"The Rock is so good, he reminds me of myself."

—*Jerry Lawler*

"He has been on more floors than Johnson's wax, but he keeps getting up."

—*Jerry Lawler*

"I smell what you're cookin'—don't smell all that good."

—*Mankind, to the Rock*

"Maybe I don't have little $500 shirts, maybe I can't raise my stupid eyebrows, and maybe I don't have 329 catchphrases."

—*Mankind, comparing himself to the Rock,*
just before a Smackdown match

"A little, insecure little man suffering from a sudden and acute attack of nontesticular fortitude."

> —*Mankind, attacking the Rock's manhood*

"Take your attitude out of my face, if you smell what the boss is cooking."

> —*Shane McMahon, to the Rock, reminding him who his father is*

"Rock, I know that you can smell that Chris Benoit will be the next World Wide Wrestling Federation Champion."

> —*Shane McMahon, just asking for a beating*

"Members are not only going to start wondering what the Rock is cooking. If you don't stop now, certain Corporate members are going to wonder what the Rock is smoking."

> —*Vince McMahon, to the Rock, who was threatening to air dirty laundry about the Corporation*

"Since I have a problem with the people, I have a problem with the people's champion."

—Vince McMahon, on the Rock

"Nickel-and-dime chump-change jabronie."

—Shawn Michaels, on the Rock

"His charisma jumped out at us."

—Kevin Misher, Universal Pictures executive, after signing the Rock to star in The Mummy II

"If you check the registry, I think you'll find that I've got reservations at the Smackdown Hotel."

—Road Dogg, just before a match with the Rock

"If anyone's going to smell what the Rock is cooking, it's gonna be me. . . . Look how big my damn nose is."

—Jason Sensation

"I've kicked your ass so many times, I'm starting to get bored with it."

—Triple H, to the Rock

"Maybe you need to switch to decaf or something."
> —*Triple H, to the Rock, who was a bit too*
> *revved up before their match*

"Stays up all night thinking of catchphrases and marketing ploys for each and every one of you."
> —*Triple H, on the Rock being too commercial*
> *and not a real wrestler*

"Hey, Rock, this was an A–B conversation. Why don't you C your way out of it."
> —*Triple H, on the Rock's mike time*

"I want you to get your TV writers that write all your comedy sketches for you, and get them to write you a eulogy."
> —*The Undertaker, just before wrestling the Rock*

"Your mouth is writing checks your ass can't cash."
> —*The Undertaker, to the Rock*

ROCK PHILOSOPHY

"Regardless of how many obstacles you throw at the Rock, regardless of what type of roadblocks you put in front of the people's champ, the Rock just keeps on coming back."

—The Rock

"They want a man who's intelligent, they want a man who's articulate, and they want a man who's pretty damn good-looking on top of all that."

—The Rock, on wrestling fans, explaining his popularity

"The Rock wipes a lobster's left testicle with what you think."

—The Rock, on a decision made by WWF commissioner Foley forcing the Rock out of the ring

"Dwayne Johnson lounges around and then takes out the garbage."

—The Rock, on his real-life personality

"Rock is a lot of things, but stink isn't one of them."
>—*The Rock, on a critic saying the Rock stinks*

"All the llamas' anuses have been licked."
>—*The Rock, another of his catchphrases*

"Dwayne Johnson with the volume turned up to its highest level and then some."
>—*The Rock, on his true identity*

DENNIS RODMAN

"One day you're passing the ball to Michael Jordan. . . . The next day you're being hit in the head with a folding chair by Professor Tanaka."
>—*Jay Leno, on Dennis Rodman's new career as professional wrestler*

"I will rip his head off and puke in the hole."
>—*Steve McMichael, on what he would do to Rodman*

"I'm gonna knock the paint right out of your hair."
> —*Diamond Dallas Page, to Rodman*

"I know that the Mailman has got a special delivery for you, Rodman."
> —*Diamond Dallas Page, on what Karl "The Mailman" Malone would do to Dennis Rodman*

"They wanted to see me get slammed, twisted, jumped on, punched, and slapped around."
> —*Dennis Rodman, on why large crowds—and many of the NBA's players—came to watch him wrestle*

"NATURE BOY" BUDDY ROGERS

"I didn't care if you loved me or hated me. What the hell's the difference? As long as you intrigued your fans."
> —*Buddy Rogers*

JIM ROSS

"You couldn't entertain a thought, much less a television audience."

> —*Jerry Lawler, to Ross, on one of his many lame comments*

"I'd like to see things from your point of view, J.R., but I'd have to get my head out of my rear end."

> —*Jerry Lawler, to Ross*

"*Old Yeller*? Is that a movie about your teeth?"

> —*Jerry Lawler, to Ross*

"I would beat up Ross, but I have a thing against cruelty to animals."

> —*Jerry Lawler*

"You have diarrhea in the mouth and constipation in the brain."

> —*Jerry Lawler, to Ross*

"That's the only exercise you get—jumping to conclusions."

—*Jerry Lawler, to Ross*

"The only exercise you get is stretching the truth."

—*Jerry Lawler, to Ross*

"I'd fire you on the spot, but I got another problem: your cohort Michael Cole sucks just as bad."

—*Shane McMahon*

"We got a real slobber-knocker here, folks."

—*Jim Ross*

ROSSATI SISTERS

"The only thing they recognize is a buffet."

—*Bobby Heenan, on the girth of the Rossati sisters*

RICK RUDE

"I look real good and feel even better. I make a burlap sack look like a cashmere sweater."

—*Rick Rude*

SABLE

"I heard she kept the BMW because it is the only one she can spell."

—*Jerry Lawler, on Sable keeping one of Triple H's cars after their breakup*

"I don't care about all the women—I only care about the men."

—*Sable, asked what she thinks the women of the WWF think about her*

"This is for the women who want to be me, and the men who come to see me."

—*Sable, her motto*

RANDY "MACHO MAN" SAVAGE

"You could pull his tongue out, and he wouldn't give up."

—*Bobby Heenan, on the indefatigable Savage*

"The computer dating service called and told me they found the perfect date for you, but the zoo would not let her out."

—*Jerry Lawler, to Savage*

"I think he's gone soft behind his woman's dress."

—*Jake Roberts, on Randy Savage hiding behind his longtime girlfriend, Elizabeth*

"Macho Madness lives forever."

—*Randy Savage, his brilliant philosophy*

ARNOLD SCHWARZENEGGER

"I know Schwarzenegger is going to be here tonight—
yeah, whoop-de-doo."

—D-Generation X, sarcastic greeting

"He's a star, but he never beat nobody up."

*—Hulk Hogan, comparing himself
to Schwarzenegger*

KEN SHAMROCK

"I will beat a lesson into you, lunkhead, that you will
never, ever forget."

—Chris Jericho, to Shamrock

"The only dangerous thing about him is to watch his
matches while operating heavy machinery."

—Chris Jericho, on the wrestling style of Shamrock

"Yeah, Twilight Zone."

—Jerry Lawler, after Jim Ross said Shamrock was in a zone

"Used to be Ken Shamrock was the world's most dangerous man, but now he's the world's most dangerous speed bump."

—Jerry Lawler

"He hit a dumbbell with a dumbbell."

—Jerry Lawler, after Owen Hart hit Shamrock with a dumbbell

"I call him the world's most dangerous butter knife."

—Jerry Lawler, on Shamrock being not so intimidating

"All you have to do with Shamrock is outsmart him, and that's not too difficult."

—Jerry Lawler

"All the times I've been hit by a chair, the one by Shamrock was the weakest, wimpiest, and wishy-washiest of them all."

—*Mankind*

"You may not be the sharpest knife in the drawer, but you're damn sure the most dangerous."

—*Vince McMahon, to Shamrock*

SGT. SLAUGHTER

"I love the scent of burnt flesh in the morning."

—*Sgt. Slaughter, parodying a line from Apocolypse Now, "I love the fresh scent of napalm in the morning."*

"The greatest living American hero."

—*Sgt. Slaughter, self-description*

AL SNOW

"I hear Al Snow is looking for me. Well, the Big Bossman is 6'7" and 310 pounds, and I'm not hard to find."

—Big Bossman

"If brains were chocolate, Al Snow's wouldn't fill an M&M."

—Jerry Lawler

"Al Snow just smelled what the Rock is cooking."

—Jerry Lawler, after the Rock pinned Snow

"Do you see any fear in the Rock's eyes over a man named Al?"

—The Rock

GEORGE "THE ANIMAL" STEELE

"Trying to referee a George Steele match is like being trapped in a steel cage with a St. Bernard."

—*Al Vass, referee*

STEINER BROTHERS

"The three toughest years of their life were the eighth grade."

—*Bobby Heenan, referring to the Steiners*

RICK STEINER

"Rick Steiner is so stupid, it takes him an hour and a half to watch *60 Minutes*."

—*Jim Cornette*

"If you don't like me, bite me."

—*Rick Steiner*

STING

"I told Sting that lump in his throat wasn't emotion—it was his liver."

—*Cactus Jack*

"He is the stupidest there ever was, the stupidest there ever is, and the stupidest there ever will be."

—*Bret Hart, on Sting*

"Sting has been stung so many times, it's getting boring."

—*Hulk Hogan*

STONE COLD PHILOSOPHY

"I like my hamburgers and beer."
—Stone Cold Steve Austin, on taking
his training very seriously

"Nobody pays back better than Steve Austin. . . .
Nobody."
—Stone Cold Steve Austin, his famous slogan

"I'll beat your ass any day of the week, twice on
weekends."
—Stone Cold Steve Austin

"Don't take this ass-whooping personally."
—Stone Cold Steve Austin, reminding an
opponent that it's all in a day's work

"I'm good at deconstructing."
—Stone Cold Steve Austin

"You can say your little prayers 24/7 and it ain't gonna save your ass from Steve Austin."

—*Stone Cold Steve Austin*

"How many people get to go to their job and beat up their boss every day?"

—*Stone Cold Steve Austin, on why he likes his job*

"Even if you've never pissed me off, you always get a payback."

—*Stone Cold Steve Austin*

"And that's the bottom line, 'cause Stone Cold said so."

—*Stone Cold Steve Austin, refusing to budge when it comes to negotiating*

"Everything we do sure hurts—but it is entertainment."

—*Stone Cold Steve Austin, evidently a man willing to suffer for his art*

"I'm pretty damn basic. The bald-headed goatee thing can be found in any mall in America."
—*Stone Cold Steve Austin, also describing most of the pro wrestling audience*

"Each and every day, I open a can of whoop-ass."
—*Stone Cold Steve Austin, on his favorite meal to serve up*

TRISH STRATUS

"Jan [the makeup lady] didn't bring the sandblaster to take away all your wrinkles."
—*Chyna, to Trish*

SUNNY

"When Sunny was in school, she wasn't very good in history, but she was great on dates."

—*Jerry Lawler*

SYXX

"He's named after his IQ or the number of brain cells he has left."

—*Jim Cornette*

TAG TEAMS

"I don't like you. The only thing I need you to do tonight is be my partner, stand on the ring apron, raise your pretty little eyebrows, and stay out of my way."

—*Big Show, to the Rock, his tag team partner for that night*

"When you play with pigs, you're going to get dirty."

> —*Bret Hart, to Randy Savage after Savage joined with Hulk Hogan and Kevin Nash*

"You shall bow in servitude after me and the Hitman kick your brains out."

> —*Hulk Hogan, to the tag team of Kevin Nash and Randy Savage*

"If there were ever two idiots who were perfect for each other, it's you two idiots."

> —*Chris Jericho, to Howard Finkel and Curtis Hughes*

"Standing in the ring together, they look like R2-D2 and C-3PO."

> —*Chris Jericho, on Kane and Chris Benoit's chemistry*

"The two biggest nerds in all of America."

> —*Chris Jericho, on the tag team of Bob Backlund and Kurt Angle*

"Personification of evil? I say personification of boredom."

—Chris Jericho, on the tag team of the Undertaker and Big Show

"This reminds me of the cantina scene from *Star Wars*."

—Chris Jericho, on the bizarre-looking Too Cool and Rikishi

"I think Blackman's in shock because he's that close to greatness."

—Jerry Lawler, on Blackman being teamed with Kurt Angle

"This is how the dinosaurs became extinct."

—Jerry Lawler, on the tag team of Moolah and Mae Young

"Like two old dinosaurs going into the La Brea Tar Pits."

—Jerry Lawler, after Jeff Jarrett pushed Moolah and Mae Young into a mud ring

"Get outta here. This isn't the rest home."

—Jerry Lawler, on the ageless Moolah
and Mae Young tag team

"There's not half a brain between them."

—Jerry Lawler, on the Mankind
and Al Snow tag team

"It was rest-home wrestling at its best."

—Jerry Lawler, on Moolah and Mae Young

"The last time Moolah and Mae went on a double date,
it was with Fred Flintstone and Barney Rubble."

—Jerry Lawler

"You should have seen what happened to them when
they went to see the Christians versus the lions."

—Jerry Lawler, on Mae and Moolah's
favorite sporting event

"I don't think these guys could warm up to each other if they were cremated together."

—*Jerry Lawler, on the Rock and Mankind and their growing friendship*

"Rock is the front end, Mankind is the rear end—but not just any rear end. Mankind is the people's rear end."

—*Mankind, on the Mankind and Rock tag team*

"I am about to serve up a giant helping of the Rock and Sock connection."

—*Mankind, on him and the Rock as a tag team*

"Neanderthal animals."

—*Vince McMahon, on Stone Cold Steve Austin and Mankind, two characters he brought to life*

"You're both something in between a cockroach and that white stuff that accumulates in the corner of your mouth when you're really, really thirsty."

—*Diamond Dallas Page, his description of the tag team of Hulk Hogan and Dennis Rodman*

"Rock and Sock, you're dumber than a bag of rocks."
—*Road Dogg, self-styled gangsta rapper*
of the pro wrestling world

"This is the Rock's hand. You don't have to like it, you don't have to respect it, all you have to do is tag it."
—*The Rock, after being teamed*
with his enemy, Triple H

"You two absolutely, unconditionally, reek of grade-A Kentucky Derby horse——."
—*The Rock, in Kentucky, to Christian and Edge*

"Teaming up with Big Show or teaming up with Big Bird, the Rock's tag team partner just don't matter to the Rock."
—*The Rock, on teaming with the Big Show*

"Is that match AARP-sanctioned?"
—*Jim Ross, on the tag team of*
Mae Young and Moolah

"This match sponsored by Geritol."

—*Jim Ross, on Brisco and Patterson wrestling together*

"Who are they going to wrestle? Mae Young and the Fabulous Moolah? They're all the same age."

—*Scott Steiner, on the tag team of Ric Flair and Hulk Hogan*

THE TANK

"I have been taking some wrestling instructions, but that won't change my strategy: to beat the hell out of my opponent until he stays down."

—*Jerry "The Tank" Bolander, espousing his unique wrestling philosophy*

TAZ

"This guy is so short, he buys an ant farm for a second
  home."

> —*Jerry Lawler, making fun of the
> vertically challenged Taz*

"He looks a lot bigger on the Lucky Charms box."

> —*Jerry Lawler*

"I have socks taller than him."

> —*Jerry Lawler*

"You may beat me—but you'll never defeat me."

> —*Taz*

TEST

"He's already had more nose jobs than Linda Tripp."
*—Jerry Lawler, preparing to do some
cosmetic surgery on Test*

"When Test was a baby, he was so ugly he had to have
tinted windows on his incubator."
—Jerry Lawler

"This guy don't know the meaning of the word *quit*. . . .
Of course, he don't know the meaning of a lot of other
words, either."
*—Jerry Lawler, whose own grammar leaves
something to be desired*

TEXAS

"I realize we're down in Texas, and not a lot of people here know where Europe is."

—*Kurt Angle, on being the European champion*

"The Rock and Texas have a lot in common. They both think they're better than everybody else."

—*Kurt Angle, on wrestling the Rock in San Antonio*

THANKSGIVING

"I am thankful for the incredible talent that I've been blessed with."

—*Kurt Angle, on Thanksgiving Day*

"The Pilgrims must be rolling over in their graves."

—*Michael Cole, on a wild WWF*
Thanksgiving Day match

"Triple H is reminiscent of a turkey here . . . getting his feathers plucked."

—*Jerry Lawler, on Triple H getting whipped on Thanksgiving Day*

"A bunch of overweight, disgusting, dysfunctional families sitting on their bums watching cartoon balloons."

—*William Regal, describing Thanksgiving in the good old USA*

THUMBS UP

"Look on the bright side—when you go to the manicurist, you can get the no-thumbs discount."

—*Chris Jericho, after he broke Chyna's thumb*

"Just shut your mouth and remember, 'thumb's the word.'"

—*Chris Jericho, to Chyna about her broken thumb*

TOOTH DECAY

"I don't make fun of you because you couldn't afford a dentist when you were growing up."

—Kurt Angle, giving dental advice to Triple H

"I hear Stu Hart goes to the dentist twice a year, once for each tooth."

—Jerry Lawler

"I don't think they are real anyway, but I don't think McMahon wants to lose them."

—Jerry Lawler, on Stone Cold's vow
to knock McMahon's teeth out

TRIPLE H

"I will hunt you down like the jackass that you are, open up a can of whoop-ass—and serve it to you right in front of the whole damn world."

> —*Stone Cold Steve Austin, to Triple H*
> *before a match*

"When I think of games, I think of tiddledywinks."

> —*Stone Cold Steve Austin, on Triple H*
> *calling himself the Game*

"It don't really matter whether you win or lose, it's how you maim the Game."

> —*Cactus Jack, whose nickname is the Game,*
> *paraphrasing a famous line to Triple H*

"I will turn you into the world's largest pincushion."

> —*Cactus Jack, to Triple H before a match*

"If I'm not mistaken, Triple H—they're calling your name."

> —*Vince McMahon, on chants of "Asshole"*
> *when Triple H was speaking*

"There are two things you can do about it: absolutely nothing and like it."

> —*The Rock, after telling Triple H*
> *how he plans to beat him*

"If you are the Game, then quite frankly you need to go back to the drawing board."

> —*The Rock, to Triple H, who said he was the Game*

"Triple H looks like Tarzan and wrestles like Jane."

> —*The Rock*

"Tonight, you're not Hunter. You are the hunted."

> —*X-Pac, to Triple H (Hunter Hearst Helmsley)*

TRIPLE H PHILOSOPHY

"While you might be a student of the game, I am the Game."

—Triple H, to Stone Cold Steve Austin

"There's not a person that can walk out here and prove to me that I'm not the very best at what I do. In this ring right now, I have no equal."

—Triple H, showing he has no problems with feelings of self-worth

"I am a God among men."

—Triple H

"The man that said you have nothing to fear but fear itself, never met me."

—Triple H

JACK TUNNEY

"He's been the best president since Noriega."
—*Bobby Heenan, on the WCW president*

TED TURNER

"I don't like Ted and he doesn't like me."
—*Vince McMahon*

MIKE TYSON

"I'll knock the damn gold teeth out of your mouth and make it into a necklace for Stone Cold."
—*Stone Cold Steve Austin, to Tyson, when Tyson was guest referee in an Austin match*

ULTIMATE WARRIOR

"He makes coffee nervous."

—*Bobby Heenan*

UNDERTAKER

"You have a spiffy little bike and some real scary
tattoos, but I don't think you have any gold medals."
—*Kurt Angle, taunting the Undertaker*

"I've been literally afraid of a man who rides a bicycle."
—*Kurt Angle, after saying he was not
afraid of the Undertaker anymore*

"Long-legged, tattooed dead man."
—*Big Show, describing the Undertaker*

"The Undertaker's gonna start a basketball team. That's for six feet and under."

—*Bobby Heenan*

"I think the Undertaker just wishes everybody were dead."

—*Jerry Lawler, on the Undertaker's attitude toward life*

"In my book, he just might be the Devil himself."
—*Vince McMahon, on the man who will never be nominated for a Good Samaritan award*

UNDERTAKER PHILOSOPHY

"Rest in peace."

—*The Undertaker, his motto*

"Embrace the darkness and relish in the unearthly delight that pain has to offer."
—*The Undertaker, what he tells his opponents*

"I have to stay with this crap for the time being."
—*The Undertaker, on how he really feels about his role as the Undertaker*

VADER

"The only time Vader sees 90210 is when he gets on the scale."
—*Jerry Lawler, on Vader's TV-viewing preferences*

"That guy eats off of satellite dishes."
—*Jerry Lawler*

"He hits you so hard, you wake up and your clothes are outta style."
—*Shawn Michaels, describing the amazing abilities of Vader*

"Vader, you're always asking what time it is. Well, it looks like Jenny Craig time to me, pal."
—*Triple H*

"You think you can play the pain game with Vader? You will lose."

> —*Vader, showing why he was the most unpopular kid on the playground*

VAL VENIS

"The single fastest up-and-coming athlete in the history of the World Wide Wrestling Federation."

> —*Val Venis, self-description*

JESSE VENTURA

"Finally, we have a governor who knows how to execute a flying head-scissors."

> —*Anonymous, on the essential qualities needed in a governor*

"Our league will be something that's not only about the best commitment to the average fan. There's Jesse Ventura."

—Dick Ebersole, president of NBC Sports, on Jesse Ventura being an announcer for the XFL

"Jesse's best move was to cheat and run."

—Hulk Hogan, speaking of both Ventura's career as a pro wrestler and his run for governor

"I'd basically stomp on him."

—Hulk Hogan, on what he would do if he got close friend Jesse Ventura in the ring

"In my business, Jesse reached about the middle of the stream. And I think in politics Jesse's probably going to go in way over his head."

—Hulk Hogan, assessing his friend Jesse Ventura's accomplishments

"I think the people of Minnesota are going to realize they made a sad mistake very soon."

—Hulk Hogan

"Combining the wise economic stewardship of Hulk Hogan and the progressive policies of Jimmy 'Superfly' Snuka."

—David Letterman, predicting how Jesse Ventura will do as Minnesota governor

"He will tell you that he never broke a rule—that's why he'll make an amazing politician."

—Dusty Rhodes, on Ventura's political prowess

"The people want someone to look up to. I'm 6'4"."

—Jesse Ventura, on why he was elected governor of Minnesota

VINCE PHILOSOPHY

"Other than being a scientist who finds a cure for some dreaded disease, the next best thing in life is entertaining the public."

—Vince McMahon

"I've never lied to any of you. I've never lied to anyone."
—Vince McMahon, proving again that honesty is the best policy

"I detest people who need help."
—Vince McMahon

"We don't pick fights. They just come along."
—Vince McMahon, refusing to take the blame for any WWF antics

"May I never, ever be thought of as legit. Anything but that."
—Vince McMahon

"A handsome, affluent entrepreneur who left his indelible mark on each and every one of you."
—Vince McMahon, on how he thinks he will be remembered

"A damned fool is someone who doesn't pucker up and kiss the boss's ass."

—*Vince McMahon, on surviving in the work world*

"A damned fool is someone who insists on doing things the hard way."

—*Vince McMahon*

VISCERA

"Viscera the Hut."

—*Chris Jericho, describing Viscera's likeness to his body double, Jabba*

"I've gotta warn you, Viscera. . . . I pity the fool who messes with Y2J."

—*Chris Jericho, sounding a lot like Mr. T*

NIKOLAI VOLKOFF

"If you hang him for being a good singer, you'd be hanging an innocent man."

—Gorilla Monsoon, on Volkoff

"In the spirit of the Geneva Summit, I am challenging the American warrior to wrestle using only science from technology."

—Nikolai Volkoff, taking a scientific, if not grammatically correct, approach to wrestling Corporal Kirchner

KOKO WARE

"Tupper."

—Bobby Heenan, guessing the name of Ware's mom

WCW

"WCW—where the big boys play . . . with each other."

—Stone Cold Steve Austin

"Look at the WWF. They don't have no old guys. We don't need no old guys. Get rid of those old sons of bitches."

—Big Poppa Pump, WCW star, on the age issue in the workplace

"Nobody watches our show anymore because it sucks too bad. I can't even watch it."

—Big Poppa Pump, on the WCW

"People see a 50-year-old man on TV, all they're going to do is change the channel to go watch the Rock, DX, or something that is cool."

—Big Poppa Pump

"I even thought about going to WCW, but I don't know if I'm quite old enough yet."

—*Mankind, looking for a place to rest his weary bones in old age*

WEIGHTY ISSUES

"Depending on how much I drink."

—*Steve Austin, asked what his weight is*

"These two guys are what a cannibal would love to get for Christmas."

—*Jerry Lawler, on Viscera and Rikishi wrestling during Christmas season*

"They looked like two fishes going after the same piece of corn."

—*Jesse Ventura, on 500-pound Uncle Elmer kissing his wife*

WHAT'S IN A NAME?

"I don't have one."

—*Goldberg, asked by Larry King*
what his first name is

"Doesn't that guy have a last name?"

—*Bobby Heenan, on Virgil*

HARVEY WIMPLEMAN

"She broke that wimp Wimpleman like a biscuit."

—*Jerry Lawler, after Jacqueline beat him up*

"There's not a woman in the world that can beat me,
'cause I'm all man."

—*Harvey Wimpleman, taking a line from*
Andy Kaufman, who was also fond
of wrestling women

WINNING

"WWF championships can be won and lost anytime—it's not like Olympic gold medals, which can forever brand you as a winner."

—Kurt Angle

"This country would be completely devastated if my streak came to an end."

—Kurt Angle, on a winning streak of his

"Everybody who's been put in my way, I've destroyed."

—Goldberg, preparing to take over the world

WORLD TOUR

"Where the hell is Samoa? Do you know? Does anybody know?"

—Eddie Guerrero, referring to Rikishi's homeland

"America—hack, pfui."

—*Iron Sheik, a true patriot*

"The country's biggest victory since the Iron Sheik pinned Sgt. Slaughter in Wrestlemania VIII."

—Jay Leno, on Iran beating the United States in soccer

"We have eclipsed you in technology. Next, we will take the Belt."

—Mr. Fuji, speaking to a group of American Steelworkers, on Japanese dominance in technology and pro wrestling

WRESTLING WISDOM

"It's not how big you are, it's how you perform in the ring."

—Lou Albano, his personal philosophy on wrestling and life

"The art of living is more like wrestling than dancing."
—*Marcus Aurelius, who, thankfully, did not live to see the transformation of wrestling over the years*

"Professional wrestling uses two of the most basic ingredients to sell its product—sex and power."
—*Dr. Mike Brannon*

"I believe that professional wrestling is clean and everything else in the world is fixed."
—*Frank Deford*

"For those who believe, no explanation is necessary. For those who don't believe, no explanation will do."
—*Jimmy Hart, who identifies with Fox Mulder on* The X-Files

"What other sport lets you kick a guy when he's down?"
—*Bobby Heenan, on wrestling*

"It's not like going to see Mike Tyson fight and he bites someone's ear off in 30 seconds. We give you two hours of energy and excitement. We give you the whole schnoz."

—Hulk Hogan

"There's no drama like wrestling."

—Andy Kaufman

"Nobody gets knifed with blood and guts hanging out. Everybody lives. We're cartoon villains."

—Stephanie McMahon

"How bad is it compared to a Schwarzenegger or Stallone movie?"

—Vince McMahon, who must wish he had Arnold and Sly on the roster

"We're storytellers. You can't just throw wrestlers out there to wrestle."

—Vince McMahon, explaining why preparation is key to wrestling

"I've adopted the same philosophy of Hollywood: Here it is—do you like it or not?"

—Vince McMahon, on the integrity of the WWF

"Soap operas for males, 18 to 34."

*—Gene Okerlund, describing the
pro wrestling demographics*

"You usually have your sports entertainment, soap opera connection. But with wrestling, you get all of this in one show."

—Steven Richards

"It bothers me when someone uses the word *fake*."

*—The Rock, after another professional
sanctioned battle*

"We are essentially a two-hour movie, minus the credits."

*—The Rock, who would know after
starring in his own movie*

"Morton Downey without words."

—*Tom Shales,* Washington Post *TV critic*

"How phony can it be if Don King isn't making any money off it?"

—Sports Illustrated, *coming to the defense of pro wrestling*

"Ballet with violence."

—*Jesse Ventura, describing pro wrestling*

"It's hip. It's exciting. It's America."

—*Andy Warhol, the king of pop culture*

WWF

"This is a mom-and-pop business. It's really a family back here."

—*Nicole Bass, on the loving WWF, which sees the Sopranos as role models*

"This is sports entertainment. This is real."

—*Chris Jericho, on the insane, unnatural,*
in-your-face world of pro wrestling

"I have no loyalty to the WWF. I've only got loyalty to good ol' J.R."

—*Jim Ross, looking out for number one*

XFL

"Have you heard about the XFL? It's like the Sopranos with helmets."

—*Jay Leno*

"There will be controversy. If there isn't, we'll create it."

—*Vince McMahon, spreading the word on the XFL*

"We understand America. We understand what America wants."

—Vince McMahon, who evidently did not understand that America did not want bad football

"You got a bunch of jockstrap-sniffing NFL team owners who don't know a damn thing about football."

—Vince McMahon, on why he can make an alternative football league succeed

"It's un-American."

—Vince McMahon, on the NFL barring football players from dating cheerleaders

"I'll now be legitimate."

—Vince McMahon, on having no predetermined winners in the XFL, as there are in pro wrestling

"The appetite isn't anywhere near satiated."

—*Vince McMahon, showing off his
amazing prediction skills*

"This won't be two massive egos clashing. Not that Dick
and I don't have massive egos."

—*Vince McMahon, on his relationship with
Dick Ebersole, president of NBC Sports*

"Vince's strategy seems to be promote the XFL like
wrestling and play it like football."

—*Neal Pilson, former CBS Sports president*

"State offices are closed on Saturdays and Sundays
anyway."

—*Jesse Ventura, on becoming an announcer
for XFL games on weekends*

"I wasn't hired because I was the governor. I was hired
because I'm Jesse the Body."

—*Jesse Ventura, on being hired
as an XFL announcer*

"We are here to have fun. It's honesty, something the media doesn't know anything about."

—*Jesse Ventura, on the XFL*

X-PAC

"The only thing I like about you is your name, 'cause it sounds almost like 'six-pack.'"

—*Stone Cold Steve Austin, to X-Pac*

"He's more nervous than a pizza on its way to Paul Bearer."

—*Jerry Lawler, on X-Pac's prematch expectation of being devoured by his opponent*

"I respect his courage. . . . It's his stupidity I have to laugh at."

—*Jerry Lawler, on X-Pac*

"You gotta stand in line to hate that guy."
>—*Jerry Lawler, on X-Pac's growing unpopularity*

"X-Pac would have been a bug on the windshield of life."
>—*Jerry Lawler, on what would have happened if X-Pac did not befriend Kane*

"He looks like a slug; that's his best natural defense."
>—*Jerry Lawler*

"If I want any crap from you, I'll pick it out of your teeth."
>—*Shawn Michaels, to X-Pac*

MAE YOUNG

"When she was in school, her teachers were the Three Wise Men."
>—*Jerry Lawler, on Young's age*

"Time may be a great healer, but it's a lousy beautician."

—*Jerry Lawler, on Young*

"When God said let there be light, Mae Young threw the switch."

—*Jerry Lawler*

"I think she got that dress originally from the real Cleopatra."

—*Jerry Lawler, on Mae Young's timeless wardrobe*

"Mae Young is so old that when David killed Goliath, she was the one that called the cops."

—*Jerry Lawler*

"Mae Young's wrinkles have wrinkles."

—*Jerry Lawler*

"Mae Young is so old, Joseph and Mary were voted cutest couple at her prom."

—Jerry Lawler

LARRY ZYBISCO

"You shut up or we'll unplug your dialysis machine, old man."

—Kevin Nash, to Zybisco

THE CLUELESS

Angle   An event or series of events that develops the program (*see* Program) or "storyline" between two or more wrestlers. Often the seed of a feud or a turn (*see* Turn). Example: Goldberg's undefeated streak was an angle that eventually led to his "retirement" from the WCW.

Babyface   A good guy. (*See* Face.) Example: The Rock is the WWF's top babyface.

Blade   To cut oneself with a concealed razor blade hidden on the wrestler him-/herself or given to the wrestler by a third party (referee, ring announcer, etc.). Usually used across the forehead. Example: I blade so much my forehead looks like a tic-tac-toe game.

Blow Up   To become extremely tired during a match. Example: Huffing and puffing more than a Hulk Hogan comeback, the wrestler was surely going to blow up.

Book   To set up the matches for the show.

Booker   The person who sets up the matches, creates the angles, writes the day's storylines, and determines their conclusions. Example: For wrestlers, the booker is the last person they want to cross before a pay-per-view event.

Bump   To fall to the mat as a result of an opponent's blow or maneuver. Example: The Spanish announcers' table is often the unacknowledged victim of a heinous bump.

Business, The   Nickname for the wrestling industry.

Call a Match   To discuss upcoming moves or spots (*see* Spot) with the other wrestler during a match. Example: The grizzled wrestler was offended that the green kid wanted to call the match, so he did the only thing he could—deliver a spine-tingling low blow.

Card   The matches for the night.

Chair Shot   A hit with a chair, usually a folding chair. Example: If you think pro wrestling is fake and no one gets hurt, take two chair shots and call me in the morning—that is, if you still have your motor skills.

Color   Blood.

Cut a Promo   To do an interview that extends an angle or program; also a chance for wrestlers to insult their opponents. Example: He cut a promo before the match, bragging about his prowess in the ring, but was silenced after his opponent rang his bell with the ring bell.

Dark Match   A match that happens before a broadcast event and is not televised. Used often as a tryout for new wrestlers.

Do the Honors   When a wrestler relinquishes his or her title by losing before leaving the promotion to put over (*see* Put Over) another remaining wrestler.

Draw   The ability of a promotion or a wrestler to bring out the fans. Example: He had as much draw as an air-conditioned igloo in the middle of a blizzard.

Face   Another word for babyface; a good guy.

Fall   When a wrestler's shoulders are held on the mat to the count of three for a loss.

Feud   A story or program between two wrestlers or a group of wrestlers (*see* Program). Example: He was in a feud with his real-life brother, which made Thanksgiving very interesting, to say the least.

Finish   The ending of a match.

Finisher   The move that earns the victory. Often wrestlers have their own signature moves as finishers—for example, Stone Cold Stunner (Stone Cold Steve Austin), the People's Elbow (the Rock).

Geek   To cut one's self.

Gimmick   The wrestler's unique character or personality. Example: With his obnoxious New Yorker gimmick, he was sure to get major heat in the South.

Green   Inexperienced.

Hardway   A cut that is not self-inflicted.

Hardway juice   A phrase describing blood produced from a cut not self-inflicted. Example: After tasting the hardway juice that oozed down his cheek, the champ got a demented smile on his face.

Heat   A negative reaction from the fans, typically boos and rude chants. Example: The top heel in the company draws the most heat.

Heel   A bad guy.

Highspot   A high-risk move, often the highlight of a match. Example: Jerry's somersault off the 20-foot ladder should have been the highspot, but a fight in the stands distracted the crowd.

Hood   A wrestler who wears a mask. Example: Being asked to wear a hood in American wrestling is usually a signal for the wrestler to seek employment elsewhere.

House Show   A wrestling show not for broadcast.

Job   A prearranged loss (*see* Put Over). Example: After doing the job and giving the rising star a push, the former champion went backstage and proceeded to beat up the booker.

Jobber   A wrestler whose main responsibility is to lose to his or her opponent and make him or her look good.

Kill   To abandon a gimmick or a match that is not getting any reaction from fans. Example: It was time to kill the costume and persona; he supposed a priest on stilts just couldn't get over with the crowd.

Main Eventer   A wrestler who is usually in the marquee matches.

Mark   A wrestling fan who thinks wrestling is real and/or takes wrestling too seriously. Example: The mark was wringing her hands, awaiting desperately the outcome of the championship match.

Marriage   A feud between wrestlers.

Midcarder   A wrestler who is well known but not used in main event matches.

Mouthpiece   A wrestler's "manager" who acts as his or her spokesperson.

No Sell   When a wrestler doesn't react to his or her opponent's blows or moves to seem invincible. Example: When his opponent diverted from their prematch plan and gave Billy's blows no sell, he decided to extract a little hardway juice from the uncooperative foe.

Over   When a wrestler's character is popular with the fans, often shown by their response when he or she comes out for a match. Example: You could tell his new persona was over when the crowd roared upon his entrance and everyone was wearing his trademark purple boa.

Paper   Complimentary tickets.

Paying Dues   To gain experience by doing jobs (*see* Job), respecting the veterans, working dark matches, etc.

Plant   Someone out in the audience posing as a fan but who gets involved in a match.

Pop   A huge, sudden reaction from the fans because of a wrestler's entrance or a spectacular move. (Also *see* Heat.)

Post   To ram someone's head or body into the ring post.

Powder Out   To get knocked out of or run out of the ring and retreat. Example: The heel tried to powder out, but the Killer dragged him back into the ring by his tights, exposing more than the crowd expected.

Program   A story between two wrestlers or group of wrestlers. (*See* Feud.)

Promoter   Head of the wrestling organization.

Promotion   A wrestling organization. Example: Across the country, small promotions can be seen performing in any type of venue, from a high school gym to an abandoned barn.

Psychology   To tell the story of the match by using well-chosen moves and working the crowd.

Push   When a wrestler is highly promoted to the fans by winning matches and titles and getting lots of airtime. Example: The bookers determined the time was ripe to push the scrawny young gun, the self-proclaimed King of the Mullets.

Put Over   When a wrestler does the job (*see* Job) and makes his or her opponent win and look good. Example: He was so good as a jobber, he could put over a blind dog with three legs if he had to.

Red   Blood.

Ring Rat   A female wrestling groupie who hopes for a sexual encounter with one of the wrestlers.

Run-In   When a person not involved in the match inter-feres. Example: She attempted to do a run-in with a chair, but her shoe heel broke and she collapsed onto the ramp.

Save   To do a run-in and rescue a wrestler who is being roughed up.

Screwjob   A controversial ending to a match, often involving underhanded tricks. Example: Fans threw empty beer cups into the ring to show their displeasure with the screwjob done to the top face.

Sell   To make it seem that an opponent's blows really hurt. Example: As much as he tried to sell the old geezer's moves, he couldn't convince a crowd that the 90-year-old man's punches actually hurt.

Sheets   Slang for publications and Internet sites that report on the "real side" of pro wrestling.

Shoot   When a match becomes a real fight, with opponents trying to legitimately hurt each other. Also means "real." Example: The wrestler broke character and did a shoot interview, challenging his former tag-team partner to meet him outside for a "talk."

Smark   A fan who thinks he or she knows everything about wrestling.

Smart   A person who knows the inside workings of pro wrestling.

Spot   A series of moves within a maneuver, usually high risk or a high point in the match. Example: He forgot the spots in the maneuver and ended up twisted in the ropes, with a groin injury as a bonus.

Stable   A group of wrestlers united in a program. Example: NWO, the Corporation, D-Generation X.

Strap   Championship belt.

Tap Out   To give up during the submission maneuver by tapping the mat. Example: The crowd roared with laughter as the wrestler realized a chimpanzee made him tap out.

Turn   To go from a villain to a good guy, or vice versa. Example: Hulk Hogan abandoned his yellow tights and did a heel turn to become the meaner Hollywood Hogan.

Tweener   A wrestler who is between being a face and a heel, usually in the process of a turn. (*See* Turn.)

Valet   A person who escorts a wrestler to the ring, often a beautiful female. Example: Miss Elizabeth was Randy "Macho Man" Savage's longtime valet and real-life wife.

Work   A ruse or ploy to fool the fans. Example: Her injury was a work to allow the wrestler some time off.

Worker   A wrestler. Example: Triple H is known as a good worker because of his ability to play up his villain-ous role.

INDEX

Italicized page numbers indicate names referred to in a quote. All other names are actual sources of a quote.